COMMON CORE

MATH

Activities that Captivate, Motivate, & Reinforce

REVISED EDITION

Grade 4

by Marjorie Frank

IncentivePublications

BY WORLD BOOK

Illustrated by Kathleen Bullock
Cover by Penny Laporte

Print Edition ISBN 978-1-62950-231-1
E-book Edition ISBN 978-1-62950-232-8 (PDF)

World Book, Inc.
180 North LaSalle Street
Suite 900
Chicago, Illinois 60601
U.S.A.

For information about World Book and Incentive Publications products, call **1-800-967-5325,** or visit our websites at **www.worldbook.com** and **www.incentivepublications.com.**

Printed in the United States of America by Mercury Print Productions, Rochester, New York

CONTENTS

Introduction

Grade 4 Common Core State Standards for Mathematics

Operations and Algebraic Thinking

Number and Operations in Base Ten

Number and Operations—Fractions

Measurement and Data

Geometry

Assessment and Answer Keys

Great Support for
Common Core State Standards!

Invite your students to join in on mysteries and adventures with colorful characters! They will delight in the high-appeal topics and engaging visuals. They can

   . . . join the world's best skiers and snowboarders to learn the latest tricks;

   . . . solve problems with real-life sports equipment and record-breaking performances;

   . . . take a walk with Olympic feet;

   . . . check out the top-performing Olympic athletes and countries;

   . . . get all the new angles on cheerleading and wrestling;

   . . . collect data on extreme onion eating, bubble blowing, and pizza tossing;

   . . . determine the fate of injured skiers;

   . . . put on a scuba tank to find deep-water solutions;

   . . . watch a champion mosquito-swatter set a new record;

   . . . and tackle many other delightful tasks.

And while they engage in these ventures, they will be moving toward competence in critical math skills, processes, and standards that they need for success in the real world.

How to Use This Book

- The pages are tools to support your teaching of the concepts, processes, and skills outlined in the Common Core State Standards. This is not a curriculum; it is a collection of engaging experiences for you to use as you do math with your students or children.

- Use any given page to introduce, explain, teach, practice, extend, assess, start a discussion about, or get students collaborating on a skill or concept.

- Use any page in a large-group or small-group setting to deepen understandings and expand knowledge or skill. Pages are not intended solely for independent work. Do them together, or always review and discuss the work together.

- Each activity is focused on a particular standard, but most make use of or can be expanded to strengthen other standards as well.

- The book is organized according to the Common Core math domains. Use the tables on pages 9 through 16 and the label at the bottom corner of each activity page to identify the standard category supported by each page.

- Use the labels on the Contents pages to see specific standards/skills for each page.

- For further mastery of Common Core State Standards for Mathematics, use the suggestions on page 8.

About Common Core State Standards for Mathematics

The Common Core State Standards for Mathematics seek to expand conceptual understanding of the key ideas of math while they strengthen foundational skills, operations, and principles. They identify what students should know, understand, and be able to do—with an emphasis on explaining principles and applying them to a wide range of situations. To best help students gain and master these robust standards. . .

1. Know the standards well. Keep them in front of you. Understand for yourself the big picture of what the standards seek to do. (See www.corestandards.org.)

2. Work to apply, expand, and deepen student skills. With activities in this book (or any learning activities), plan to include

   . . . interaction with peers in pairs, small groups, and large groups.

   . . . plenty of discussion, integration, and hands-on work with math concepts.

   . . . emphasis on questioning, analyzing, modeling math situations, explaining what you are doing and thinking, using tools effectively, and applying to real world problems.

   . . . lots of observation, meaningful feedback, follow-up, and reflection.

3. Ask questions that advance reasoning, application, and real-life connection:

   - *What, exactly, IS the problem?*
   - *Can you solve this another way?*
   - *Does this make sense? (Why or why not?)*
   - *Can you state the problem in a different way?*
   - *What information is needed to solve this problem?*
   - *What information in the problem is not needed?*
   - *What operations do you need to use?*
   - *If we change ____, what will happen to ____?*
   - *What tools do you need to solve this?*
   - *Can you draw your problem-solving process?*
   - *What did you learn from solving this problem?*
   - *When could you use this? Where could you use this?*
   - *Now that you know how to ____, where can you use this?*
   - *How did you arrive at your answer?*
   - *How can you show that your answer is right?*
   - *Where else have you seen a problem like this?*
   - *What does this ask you to do?*
   - *What led you to this conclusion?*
   - *How could we figure this out?*
   - *What was the first step you took?*
   - *What information is missing?*
   - *How could you make a model of this?*
   - *How could you draw your solution?*
   - *How do you know this is right?*
   - *What patterns do you notice?*
   - *Where have you seen this in real life?*
   - *What does this remind you of?*
   - *Could there be another answer?*
   - *If this is true, what else might be true?*
   - *How can you explain your answer?*
   - *Could you ask that question differently?*
   - *What will you do next?*

Standards for Mathematical Practice

St. #	Standard	Pages in This Book
CCSS.MP1	Make sense of problems and persevere in solving them.	18-34, 36-54, 56-84, 86-109, 112-126
CCSS.MP2	Reason abstractly and quantitatively.	18-34, 36-54, 56-84, 86-109, 112-126
CCSS.MP3	Construct viable arguments and critique the reasoning of others.	18-34, 36-54, 56-84, 86-109, 112-126
CCSS.MP4	Model with mathematics.	18-34, 36-54, 56-84, 86-109, 112-126
CCSS.MP5	Use appropriate tools strategically.	18-34, 36-54, 56-84, 86-109, 112-126
CCSS.MP6	Attend to precision.	18-34, 36-54, 56-84, 86-109, 112-126
CCSS.MP7	Look for and make use of structure.	32–34, 36–44, 56–59, 62–76, 77–84, 94–95, 102–110, 112–126
CCSS.MP8	Look for and express regularity in repeated reasoning.	18–28, 45–54, 56–59, 81–84, 86–93

Grade 4 Common Core State Standards for Mathematical Content

4.OA   Operations and Algebraic Thinking

St. #	Standard	Pages in This Book
Use the four operations with whole numbers to solve problems.		
4.OA.A.1	Interpret a multiplication equation as a comparison, e.g., interpret $35 = 5 \times 7$ as a statement that 35 is 5 times as many as 7 and 7 times as many as 5. Represent verbal statements of multiplicative comparisons as multiplication equations.	18, 19, 20-21, 24, 25, 26, 27, 28
4.OA.A.2	Multiply or divide to solve word problems involving multiplicative comparison, e.g., by using drawings and equations with a symbol for the unknown number to represent the problem, distinguishing multiplicative comparison from additive comparison.	20-21, 22, 23
4.OA.A.3	Solve multistep word problems posed with whole numbers and having whole-number answers using the four operations, including problems in which remainders must be interpreted. Represent these problems using equations with a letter standing for the unknown quantity. Assess the reasonableness of answers using mental computation and estimation strategies including rounding.	20-21, 23, 24, 25, 26, 27-28, 52
Gain familiarity with factors and multiples.		
4.OA.B.4	Find all factor pairs for a whole number in the range 1–100. Recognize that a whole number is a multiple of each of its factors. Determine whether a given whole number in the range 1–100 is a multiple of a given one-digit number. Determine whether a given whole number in the range 1–100 is prime or composite.	29, 30, 31
Generate and analyze patterns.		
4.OA.C.5	Generate a number or shape pattern that follows a given rule. Identify apparent features of the pattern that were not explicit in the rule itself. *For example, given the rule "Add 3" and the starting number 1, generate terms in the resulting sequence and observe that the terms appear to alternate between odd and even numbers. Explain informally why the numbers will continue to alternate in this way.*	32, 33, 34

10

Grade 4 Common Core State Standards for Mathematical Content

4.NBT   Number and Operations in Base Ten

St. #	Standard	Pages in This Book
Generalize place value understanding for multi-digit whole numbers.		
4.NBT.A.1	Recognize that in a multi-digit whole number, a digit in one place represents ten times what it represents in the place to its right. *For example, recognize that 700 ÷ 70 = 10 by applying concepts of place value and division.*	36-37, 38, 39, 40, 41
4.NBT.A.2	Read and write multi-digit whole numbers using base-ten numerals, number names, and expanded form. Compare two multi-digit numbers based on meanings of the digits in each place, using >, =, and < symbols to record the results of comparisons.	36-37, 38, 39, 40, 41, 42, 43, 44
4.NBT.A.3	Use place value understanding to round multi-digit whole numbers to any place.	42, 43, 44
Use place value understanding and properties of operations to perform multi-digit arithmetic.		
4.NBT.B.4	Fluently add and subtract multi-digit whole numbers using the standard algorithm.	45, 46, 47, 48, 54
4.NBT.B.5	Multiply a whole number of up to four digits by a one-digit whole number, and multiply two two-digit numbers, using strategies based on place value and the properties of operations. Illustrate and explain the calculation by using equations, rectangular arrays, and/or area models.	48, 49, 50, 51, 54
4.NBT.B.6	Find whole-number quotients and remainders with up to four-digit dividends and one-digit divisors, using strategies based on place value, the properties of operations, and/or the relationship between multiplication and division. Illustrate and explain the calculation by using equations, rectangular arrays, and/or area models.	48, 51, 52, 53, 54

Common Core Reinforcement Activities — 4th Grade Math

Grade 4 Common Core State Standards for Mathematical Content

4.NF   Number and Operations—Fractions

St. #	Standard	Pages in This Book
Extend understanding of fraction equivalence and ordering.		
4.NF.A.1	Explain why a fraction *a/b* is equivalent to a fraction *(n × a)/(n × b)* by using visual fraction models, with attention to how the number and size of the parts differ even though the two fractions themselves are the same size. Use this principle to recognize and generate equivalent fractions.	56, 57, 58, 59
4.NF.A.2	Compare two fractions with different numerators and different denominators, e.g., by creating common denominators or numerators, or by comparing to a benchmark fraction such as $\frac{1}{2}$. Recognize that comparisons are valid only when the two fractions refer to the same whole. Record the results of comparisons with symbols >, =, or <, and justify the conclusions, e.g., by using a visual fraction model.	58, 59
Build fractions from unit fractions by applying and extending previous understandings of operations on whole numbers.		
4.NF.B.3	Understand a fraction *a/b* with *a* > 1 as a sum of fractions 1/*b*.	60-68
4.NF.B.3a	Understand addition and subtraction of fractions as joining and separating parts referring to the same whole.	60, 61, 62, 63, 64, 65, 66, 67, 68, 69
4.NF.B.3b	Decompose a fraction into a sum of fractions with the same denominator in more than one way, recording each decomposition by an equation. Justify decompositions, e.g., by using a visual fraction model.	60, 61, 62, 63, 64, 65, 66, 67, 68, 69
4.NF.B.3c	Add and subtract mixed numbers with like denominators, e.g., by replacing each mixed number with an equivalent fraction, and/or by using properties of operations and the relationship between addition and subtraction.	63, 64, 65, 66, 67, 68, 69
4.NF.B.3d	Solve word problems involving addition and subtraction of fractions referring to the same whole and having like denominators, e.g., by using visual fraction models and equations to represent the problem.	65, 66, 67, 68

Grade 4 Common Core State Standards for Mathematical Content

4.NF   Number and Operations—Fractions, continued

St. #	Standard	Pages in This Book
4.NF.B.4	Apply and extend previous understandings of multiplication to multiply a fraction by a whole number.	70-76
4.NF.B.4a	Understand a multiple of a/b as a multiple. Understand a fraction *a/b* as a multiple of 1/*b*. *For example, use a visual fraction model to represent 5/4 as the product 5 × (1/4), recording the conclusion by the equation 5/4 = 5 × (1/4).*	70, 71
4.NF.B.4b	Understand a multiple of a/b as a multiple of 1/b, and use this understanding to multiply a fraction by a whole number. *For example, use a visual fraction model to express 3 × (2/5) as 6 × (1/5), recognizing this product as 6/5. (In general, n × (a/b) = (n × a)/b.)*	72, 73
4.NF.B.4c	Measure to determine how much longer one object is than another object. Solve word problems involving multiplication of a fraction by a whole number, e.g., by using visual fraction models and equations to represent the problem. *For example, if each person at a party will eat 3/8 of a pound of roast beef, and there will be 5 people at the party, how many pounds of roast beef will be needed? Between what two whole numbers does your answer lie?*	74, 75, 76
	Understand decimal notation for fractions, **and compare decimal fractions.**	
4.NF.C.5	Express a fraction with denominator 10 as an equivalent fraction with denominator 100, and use this technique to add two fractions with respective denominators 10 and 100. *For example, express 3/10 as 30/100, and add 3/10 + 4/100 = 34/100.*	77, 78, 79, 80, 81, 82, 83, 84
4.NF.C.6	Use decimal notation for fractions with denominators 10 or 100. *For example, rewrite 0.62 as 62/100; describe a length as 0.62 meters; locate 0.62 on a number line diagram.*	77, 78, 79, 80, 81, 82, 83, 84
4.NF.C.7	Compare two decimals to hundredths by reasoning about their size. Recognize that comparisons are valid only when the two decimals refer to the same whole. Record the results of comparisons with the symbols >, =, or <, and justify the conclusions, e.g., by using a visual model.	81, 82, 83, 84

Grade 4 Common Core State Standards for Mathematical Content

4.MD   Measurement and Data

St. #	Standard	Pages in This Book
Solve problems involving measurement and conversion of measurements from a larger unit to a smaller unit.		
4.MD.A.1	Know relative sizes of measurement units within one system of units including km, m, cm; kg, g; lb, oz.; l, ml; hr, min, sec. Within a single system of measurement, express measurements in a larger unit in terms of a smaller unit. Record measurement equivalents in a two-column table. *For example, know that 1 ft is 12 times as long as 1 in. Express the length of a 4 ft snake as 48 in. Generate a conversion table for feet and inches listing the number pairs (1, 12), (2, 24), (3, 36), . . .*	86, 87, 88, 89, 90
4.MD.A.2	Use the four operations to solve word problems involving distances, intervals of time, liquid volumes, masses of objects, and money, including problems involving simple fractions or decimals, and problems that require expressing measurements given in a larger unit in terms of a smaller unit. Represent measurement quantities using diagrams such as number line diagrams that feature a measurement scale.	86, 87, 88, 89, 90, 91, 92, 93, 94
4.MD.A.3	Apply the area and perimeter formulas for rectangles in real world and mathematical problems. *For example, find the width of a rectangular room given the area of the flooring and the length, by viewing the area formula as a multiplication equation with an unknown factor.*	86, 87, 88, 89, 90, 94-95, 96
Represent and interpret data.		
4.MD.B.4	Make a line plot to display a data set of measurements in fractions of a unit ($\frac{1}{2}$, $\frac{1}{4}$, $\frac{1}{8}$). Solve problems involving addition and subtraction of fractions by using information presented in line plots. *For example, from a line plot find and interpret the difference in length between the longest and shortest specimens in an insect collection.*	97, 98, 99, 100-101

Grade 4 Common Core State Standards for Mathematical Content

4.MD   Measurement and Data, continued

St. #	Standard	Pages in This Book
	Geometric measurement: understand concepts of angle and measure angles.	
4.MD.C.5	Recognize angles as geometric shapes that are formed wherever two rays share a common endpoint, and understand concepts of angle measurement.	102-110
4.MD.C.5a	An angle is measured with reference to a circle with its center at the common endpoint of the rays, by considering the fraction of the circular arc between the points where the two rays intersect the circle. An angle that turns through 1/360 of a circle is called a "one-degree angle," and can be used to measure angles.	102-103, 104, 105, 106-107, 108, 109, 110
4.MD.C.5b	An angle that turns through n one-degree angles is said to have an angle measure of n degrees.	102-103, 104, 105, 106-107, 108, 109, 110
4.MD.C.6	Measure angles in whole-number degrees using a protractor. Sketch angles of specified measure.	102-103, 104, 106-107, 108, 109, 110
4.MD.C.7	Recognize angle measure as additive. When an angle is decomposed into non-overlapping parts, the angle measure of the whole is the sum of the angle measures of the parts. Solve addition and subtraction problems to find unknown angles on a diagram in real world and mathematical problems, e.g., by using an equation with a symbol for the unknown angle measure.	106-107, 108, 109, 110

Grade 4 Common Core State Standards for Mathematical Content

4.G   Geometry

St. #	Standard	Pages in This Book
Draw and identify lines and angles, and classify shapes by properties of their lines and angles.		
4.G.A.1	Draw points, lines, line segments, rays, angles (right, acute, obtuse), and perpendicular and parallel lines. Identify these in two-dimensional figures.	112, 113, 114, 115, 116
4.G.A.2	Classify two-dimensional figures based on the presence or absence of parallel or perpendicular lines, or the presence or absence of angles of a specified size. Recognize right triangles as a category, and identify right triangles.	117, 118, 119, 120, 121
4.G.A.3	Recognize a line of symmetry for a two-dimensional figure as a line across the figure such that the figure can be folded along the line into matching parts. Identify line-symmetric figures and draw lines of symmetry.	122, 123, 124, 125, 126

OPERATIONS
AND
ALGEBRAIC
THINKING

Grade 4

PRACTICE MAKES PERFECT

Olympic athletes practice for hours. These hours add up to weeks, months, and even years! Practice your multiplication skills. Fill in the missing numbers in each statement.

1. _____ is 4 times as many as 8 and 8 times as many as 4.

2. 9 times as many as 6 and 6 times as many as 9 is _____ .

3. _____ is 12 times as many as 2 and 2 times as many as 12.

4. 48 is _____ times as many as 8 and 8 times as many as _____ .

5. _____ is 7 times as many as 9 and 9 times as many as 7.

6. _____ is 4 times as many as 7 and 7 times as many as _____ .

7. _____ is 9 times as many as 5 and 5 times as many as 9.

8. 56 is _____ times as many as 7 and 7 times as many as _____ .

Name _____

GETTING TO VENUES

A venue is a place where an Olympic event is held. There are many different venues at the Olympic Games. These athletes are heading for their venues, but their paths are blocked. Remove obstacles by finishing the math equations.

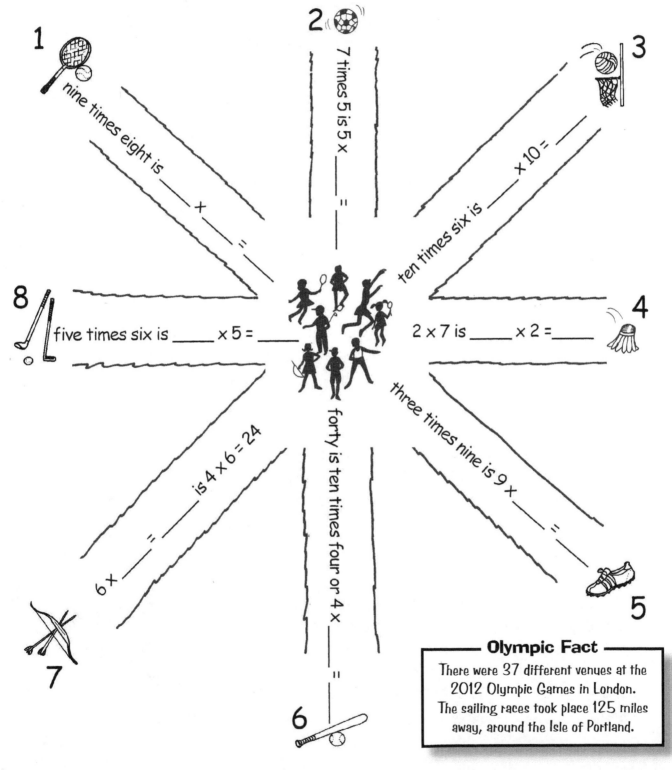

1 nine times eight is _____ + _____ = _____

2 7 times 5 is 5 x _____ = _____

3 ten times six is _____ x 10 = _____

8 five times six is _____ x 5 = _____

4 2 x 7 is _____ x 2 = _____

5 three times nine is 9 x _____ = _____

7 6 x _____ = _____ is 4 x 6 = 24

6 forty is ten times four or 4 x _____ = _____

Olympic Fact

There were 37 different venues at the 2012 Olympic Games in London. The sailing races took place 125 miles away, around the Isle of Portland.

Name

WINTER SPORTS FEST

Every winter the Bigtown Middle School has a Winter Sports Fest. Students take part in all kinds of sports—from ski races and ice-carving contests to snowball-throwing competitions.

Solve the problems on this page and the next (page 21) about the Sports Fest.
In each equation, **n** = the missing number. Circle the correct equation for each problem. Then give the value of **n**.

1. Student athletes drank 500 cups of hot chocolate during the sports fest. They each drank 5 cups. How many athletes were in the contests?

   a. **500 x 5 = n**   b. **500 + 5 = n**   c. **5 x n = 500**

   n = _____

2. Tanisha threw a snowball 48 feet. This was four times as far as Josh's best throw. How far did Josh throw the snowball?

   a. **48 ÷ 4 = n**   b. **4 x 48 = n**   c. **48 − n = 4**

   n = _____

3. 30 spectators attended the toboggan race. 180 watched the speed skating event. How many times more spectators watched speed skating than toboggan racing?

   a. **180 − n = 30**   b. **180 ÷ n = 30**   c. **30 x 180 = n**

   n = _____

4. The warmest temperature of the weekend was Saturday morning. By the end of the day, the temperature had fallen to half of that amount: 15°F. What was the Saturday morning temperature?

   a. **n ÷ 2 = 15**   b. **15 ÷ 2 = n**   c. **n + 2 = 15**

   n = _____

Use with page 21.

Name

Word Problems; Multiplication and Division

Read about these activities at the Winter Sports Fest. Follow the directions in each problem to write an equation that will lead to the answer. Use **n** to represent the missing number. Solve the equation for the missing number **n**.

5. Winn and Lucas finished second in the two-person sled race with a time of 220 seconds. This time was twice the time of the winners. What was the time of the first-place team?

   Write a multiplication equation that solves the problem.

   _____   **n** = _____

6. About 20 pounds of ice were used for each ice sculpture. A total of 260 pounds of ice were used in the entire competition. How many ice sculptures were created?

   Write a division equation that solves the problem.

   _____   **n** = _____

7. There were a total of 480 falls during the snowboarding competition. Each team, on average, had 24 falls. How many teams participated?

   Write a division equation that solves the problem.

   _____   **n** = _____

8. At the award ceremony, 150 awards were given out. This was three times as many as last year. How many awards were given last year?

   Write a multiplication equation that solves the problem.

   _____   **n** = _____

Use with page 20.

Name _____

Common Core Reinforcement Activities — 4th Grade Math

TRICKS GALORE

Wild Will has perfected a long list of snowboard tricks. Let's hope he can pull them off in this competition! Read the tales about his practice and competition. Find the value of the missing number (**n**) to solve each problem.

1. What a great day I have had! I got 12 first place finishes. This is 4 times as many first place finishes as last year. How many times did I finish first last year?

    4n = 12   n = _____

2. In practice, I did 200 Ollies and 400 Fakies. I did twice as many Tail Rolls as these other two tricks combined. How many Tail Rolls did I practice?

    2(200 + 400) = n   n = _____

3. I ate 28 energy bars this week. That is 7 times as many as I usually eat in a week. How many do I usually eat?

    28 ÷ n = 7   n = _____

4. After my last competition, I had 60 bruises on my body. This was 5 times the number of scrapes I got today. How many scrapes did I get today?

    5n = 60   n = _____

5. So far this year, I have spent $440 on passes to the ski hill to practice. Each time I go, I spend $4 on a pass. How many times have I been to the hill?

    440 ÷ 4 = n   n = _____

6. I have practiced a total of 360 hours so far this season. I have been to the park 120 times. How many hours have I practiced each time?

    120n = 360   n = _____

Name

22

SOMETHING'S MISSING

When Sheira heads down the slope, it's hard to get her to stop—even though she is missing something important! Something is also missing in each of these equations, too. For each problem, find the value of the missing number (**n**).

1. The wind at the top of the hill is 15 mph. Sheira skis down the mountain at 30 mph. How many times faster is the speed of the wind than Sheira's speed?

   15n = 30   n = _____

2. There are 4,800 skiers on the slopes at Holiday Hollow today. Of these, 600 are expert skiers. How many times more non-expert skiers are on the hill than experts?

   600n = 4,800   n = _____

3. A new skier, Alexa, fell 36 times during a 3-hour lesson. She fell the same number of times each hour. How many times did she fall each hour?

   36 ÷ 3 = n   n = _____

4. Last season, 400,000 tickets were sold at Holiday Hollow Ski Resort. In the first month of this season, 8,000 have been sold. How many times more tickets were sold in the entire season last year?

   400,000 ÷ n = 8,000   n = _____

5. Sheira spent $1,950 on ski equipment. She spent a third that much on ski clothing. How much did she spend on clothing?

   1,950 ÷ 3 = n   n = _____

6. The ski patrol rescues many skiers in trouble each day. Of those rescued last week, 88 had broken bones. Nine times that many had sprained ankles or wrists. How many had sprains?

   88 x 9 = n   n = _____

7. Sheira won several slalom races this year. Toya won twice as many. Lucia has won twice as many as Toya. All together the three girls won 56 races. How many races did Sheira win?

   n + 2n + 2(2n) = 56   n = _____

Name _____

Common Core Reinforcement Activities — 4th Grade Math

GREAT FANS

The Slicksville fans are all wound up today. Their baseball team is on a 20-game winning streak. Solve their baseball game problems. Be alert! These problems will take more than one step to solve. Solve each problem for the missing number, **n**.

1. Bud, the hot dog vendor, sells 2 sizes of dogs. At Friday's game, he sold 28 junior dogs and 56 jumbo dogs at $4 each. He took in a total of $308. How much did each junior dog cost?

    28n + (56 x 4) = 308

    n = _____

2. Red McGrew is having a great game. He hit a single. (He got to first base.) He hit a double. (He ran to first, then to second base.) He got a triple. (He ran to first, second, and then third base.) He ran a total of 540 feet on these hits. How far apart were the bases?

    n + 2n + 3n = 540

    n = _____

3. Lou's grandpa took his family to the game today. He started with $60. He bought a senior ticket for $5, two adult tickets, and four children's tickets at $2 each. He had $33 left for snacks. How much did each adult ticket cost?

    60 – 5 – 2n – (4 x 2) = 33

    n = _____

4. During fifth inning, it started raining. Luckily Rosa brought 3 umbrellas, 2 slickers, and 4 plastic garbage bags. The bags and slickers were good to each cover one friend. She helped 14 friends (plus herself) stay dry. How many people did each umbrella cover?

    3n + 2 + 4 = 14 + 1

    n = _____

5. Salina and her 18 friends all want to sit together in the bleachers. They found 2 rows with 4 seats each and 2 rows with 3 seats each. How many more seats will they need to find?

    (2 x 4) + (2 x 3) + n = 18

    n = _____

6. The Slicksville Booster Club sells programs at home games. They want to raise $6,500 for a new scoreboard. As of tonight, they have raised $5,000. There are 5 home games left in the season. How much do they need to raise at each remaining game?

    $$\frac{(6,500 - 5,000)}{5} = n$$

    n = _____

Name _____

SINK THAT BASKET

The Panthers and Tigers are big rivals. This game will decide the championship.

Circle the correct equation to represent each problem. Then solve the problem to find **n**.

1. In the first half, the Tigers scored eight 2-point baskets, 7 foul shots for 1 point each, and several 3-point baskets. At the end of the quarter, their score was 38. How many 3-point shots did they make?

   a. $8 + 7 + n = 38$ b. $(8 \times 2) + 7 + 3n = 38$ c. $38 - 3n - 7 = (2 \times 8)$

   n = _____

2. At the end of the championship game, the Panthers had scored the same number of points as in each of their previous two games. The total of these was 189 points. What was the Panthers' score in the championship game?

   a. $189 = 3n$ b. $189 = \frac{3}{n}$ c. $189 - 2n = n$

   n = _____

3. To get to the game, the Panthers traveled 4 times as far as the Tigers. The Panthers traveled 128 miles. How far did the Tigers travel?

   a. $(4 \times 128) = n$ b. $n = (128 \div 4)$ c. $n + 4 = 128$

   n = _____

4. A typical player breathes seven quarts of air a minute while sitting on the bench and 20 times that much per minute while playing a strenuous game. If Lucinda played for 20 minutes and sat on the bench for 10 minutes, how many quarts of air did she breathe during the 30-minute game?

   a. $20 + 7 + 22 + 10 + 32 = n$
   b. $32 = n = 7$
   c. $(20 \times 140) + (10 \times 7) = n$

   n = _____

5. Player Shaundra Peters dribbled the basketball a total distance of 3,788 feet during the game. Her sister Denise dribbled the ball 894 feet fewer than half Shaundra's distance. How far did Denise dribble?

   a. $3788 - 894 = n$ b. $3788 - n = 894$ c. $(3788 \div 2) - 894 = n$

   n = _____

Name _____

BUMPS, BRUISES, AND BREAKS

In every game, somebody on the Bloombury Bruins Hockey Team gets injured. The team members have solved some problems about their injuries.

Use mental math and estimation to decide if each answer is reasonable. Write **yes** or **no**.

Is the answer reasonable?

_____ 1. The cost of hospital trips for the team members averages $200,000 a season. The season is five months long. The team has 40 players. Players figure $1000 is spent each month on each player for hospital costs.

_____ 2. Thomas and Georgio each bumped his shins an average of 30 times in each period of tonight's game. Each of these 2 players also bruised his nose 20 times in each period. There are 3 periods in the game. They calculated that the two of them got a total of 3000 bumps and bruises in the game.

_____ 3. Last season, Louis and Ramon each had a total of 150 injuries between them. They had 40 broken teeth, 30 black eyes, and 25 torn ligaments. The rest of the injuries were cuts and bruises. Louis says they had 50 cuts and 100 bruises.

_____ 4. The Bruins had an average of 25 injuries in each game. They played 8 games. One-tenth of the injuries were sprains. The coach figured that there were 20 sprains.

_____ 5. About 20 players are hit in the upper body with a hockey puck some time during each game. The Bruins played 8 games. The coach says it is possible that a player can go the whole season without being hit by a puck.

Name _____

THE FINAL COUNT

A total of 958 medals were awarded at the 2008 Summer Olympic Games in Bejing, China. Here is the final medal count for the top 20 medal-winning countries.

Summer Olympic Games 2008
Final Medal Count for Top 20 Countries

Country	Gold	Silver	Bronze	Total
USA	36	38	36	110
China	51	21	28	100
Russia	23	21	29	73
Great Britain	19	13	15	47
Australia	14	15	17	46
Germany	16	10	15	41
France	7	16	18	41
South Korea	13	10	8	31
Italy	8	9	10	27
Ukraine	7	5	15	27
Japan	9	6	10	25
Cuba	2	11	11	24
Belarus	4	5	10	19
Spain	5	10	3	18
Canada	3	9	6	18
Netherlands	7	5	4	16
Brazil	3	4	8	15
Kenya	6	4	4	14
Kazakhstan	2	4	7	13
Jamaica	6	3	2	11

Use the information from the chart to decide if the statements below make sense. Write **yes** or **no**. Use mental math and estimation.

_____ 1. The top five countries won more total silver medals than gold medals.

_____ 2. Ten countries won about four times the number of medals as Japan.

_____ 3. The 11th through 20th countries won three times as many bronze medals as gold medals.

_____ 4. Neither Brazil nor Kenya won one-fourth as many gold medals as China.

_____ 5. Jamaica won about 100 medals fewer than the USA.

_____ 6. Australia won three times as many silver medals as Belarus, Ukraine, or Netherlands.

_____ 7. Russia won about 9 times as many gold and silver medals (total) as Spain.

_____ 8. France and Italy combined won a number of total medals that equaled the gold medals of China.

_____ 9. Great Britain won about the same number of gold and silver medals combined as Cuba.

_____ 10. The top three countries won a total of medals that was about seven times the total of countries 18, 19, and 20.

Name

A total of 258 medals were awarded at the 2010 Winter Olympic Games in Vancouver, British Columbia, Canada. Here is the final medal count for the top 10 medal-winning countries.

Use the information from the chart to decide if the statements below make sense. Write **yes** or **no**. Use mental math and estimation.

Winter Olympic Games 2010
Final Medal Count for Top 10 Countries

Country	Gold	Silver	Bronze	Total
USA	9	15	13	37
Germany	10	13	7	30
Canada	14	7	5	26
Norway	9	8	6	23
Austria	4	6	6	16
Russia	3	5	7	15
South Korea	6	6	2	14
China	5	2	4	11
Sweden	5	2	4	11
France	2	3	6	11

_____ 1. Germany's medal count was three times that of France's less three.

_____ 2. The top four countries won about 10 times as many medals total as the total of the next six countries.

_____ 3. The top ten countries won fewer than 30 bronze medals total.

_____ 4. Together, Sweden and China won about as many gold medals as the total of silver medals won by the United States and Germany.

_____ 5. Russia won half as many medals as Germany.

_____ 6. Austria's total medal count was half of the USA's silver medal count.

_____ 7. Austria won about 30 medals fewer than Canada.

_____ 8. South Korea's gold and silver total was equal to Russia's silver and bronze total.

_____ 9. France's total was more than one-third of Germany's total.

_____ 10. Norway's total medal count was close to the medal count of Canada's gold and silver combined.

Name

EXPLOSIVE SPEEDS

People began sledding over 15,000 years ago on sleds made of a strip of animal skin stretched between two pieces of wood. These days, Olympic bobsleds are high-tech machines made for speed. Bobsledding is thrilling to watch! A crew of two or four flies down a mile-long, curvy course at speeds of more than 120 mph.

Olympic Fact

It never snows in Jamaica. The average temperature is 80°! Even so, Jamaica has a bobsled team. In the 1994 Winter Olympics, Jamaica's team finished 14th—ahead of both U.S. teams!

See how fast you can find factors for these bobsleds. Write four factors for the number on the front of the sled. Write one factor on the helmet of each crew member.

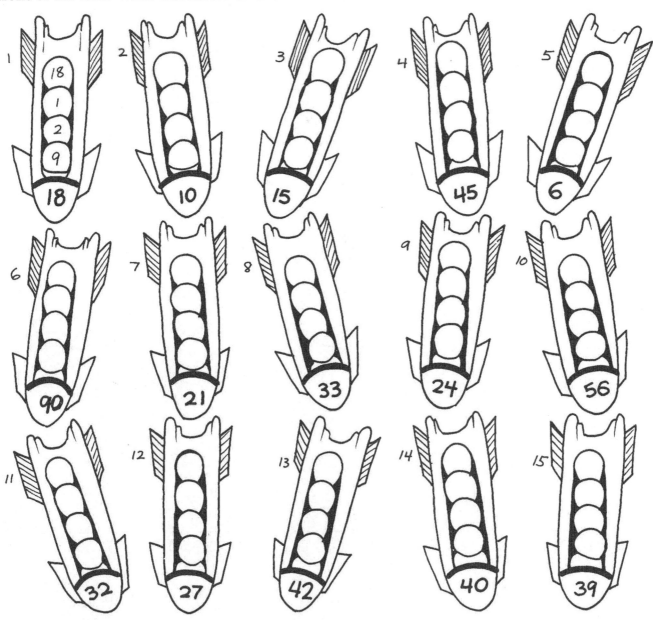

Go back and color the helmet for any prime factor.

Name _____

NO BRAKES!

It is said that some of the earliest bobsleds had no brakes and were steered by a rope! The sleds were stopped in a very interesting way. Find out how by solving the puzzle below.

Write the greatest common factor for each pair of numbers. Then write the corresponding letter to your answer on the line above that answer in the puzzle at the bottom of the page. If your answers are correct, you will find out how the sleds were stopped.

1. 2 and 4 _____ R

2. 9 and 6 _____ E

3. 11 and 33 _____ T

4. 14 and 28 _____ I

5. 30 and 45 _____ V

6. 18 and 24 _____ N

7. 28 and 32 _____ D

8. 15 and 27 _____ E

9. 80 and 50 _____ A

10. 12 and 36 _____ K

11. 3 and 9 _____ E

12. 4 and 12 _____ D

13. 6 and 10 _____ R

14. 16 and 6 _____ R

15. 14 and 10 _____ R

16. 10 and 40 _____ A

17. 5 and 25 _____ G

18. 15 and 50 _____ G

19. 16 and 4 _____ D

20. 7 and 35 _____ H

21. 12 and 32 _____ D

22. 40 and 90 _____ A

23. 5 and 15 _____ G

24. 20 and 10 _____ A

25. 22 and 6 _____ R

26. 15 and 9 _____ E

27. 21 and 3 _____ E

_____ _____ _____   _____ _____ _____ _____ _____ _____   _____ _____ _____ _____ _____ _____ _____
11   7   3   4   2   14   15   3   2   4   2   10   5   5   3   4

_____   _____ _____ _____ _____ _____ _____   _____ _____ _____ _____   to stop the sled.
10   5   10   2   4   3   6   2   10   12   3

Name _____

OUTLANDISH COMPETITIONS

There are some very strange competitions out there! It is quite amazing what things people think of to eat, balance, throw, juggle, build, and race! Here are a few of the real things people do for fun to try to set new records for how many, how long, or how far they can do something.

The table shows the number of competitors for each of four years. Someone counted the number of people that participated in each contest. The numbers were put into this **frequency table**. It shows how frequently an onion eater, shoe shiner, or other competitor was counted.

Wild and Wacky Competitions Frequency of Registrations				
Competition	Year 1	Year 2	Year 3	Year 4
a. Pizza Tossers	53	18	45	50
b. Watermelon Seed Spitters	36	72	26	35
c. Onion Eaters	14	22	46	17
d. Elephant Lifters	3	2	0	8
e. Egg Balancers	27	42	19	54
f. Bubble Blowers	31	17	14	13
g. Mosquito Killers	82	50	68	11
h. Wall Sitters	29	13	71	47
i. Lemon Eaters	95	15	20	30
j. Bed Makers	36	54	15	18
k. Shoe Shiners	26	14	19	12
l. Sand Castle Builders	10	20	35	46
m. Flaming Torch Jugglers	60	35	85	5

Use the table to answer the questions.

1. Which competitions show all multiples of 5? _____

2. Which shows all composite numbers? (Circle one.)

   a. Elephant Lifters

   b. Shoe Shiners

   c. Sand Castle Builders

3. How many competitions show numbers that are all multiples of 2? _____

4. Which competitions include multiples of 12? _____

5. Which competition shows all prime numbers? _____

6. Which includes only one prime number? (Circle one or more.)

   a. Shoe Shiners

   b. Pizza Tossers

   c. Onion Eaters

7. How many composite numbers are in the Bubble Blowers data? _____

8. Which competition numbers are all multiples of 3? _____

Name _____

Common Core Reinforcement Activities — 4th Grade Math

SWATTING TO SET A RECORD

Yes, there really is a World Mosquito-Killing Championship. It is held every year in Finland. Henri Pellonpää holds the record for the most of the pesky insects killed in five minutes. His record is 21 mosquitoes.

Find and finish the patterns to solve problems about more mosquito swatting.

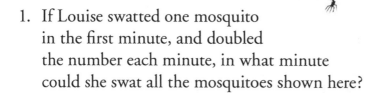

1. If Louise swatted one mosquito in the first minute, and doubled the number each minute, in what minute could she swat all the mosquitoes shown here?

2. On one day, Louise swatted 150 mosquitoes. On the next day, she swatted 120. On Day 4 she swatted 60, and on Day 6 she swatted none. What is the pattern of her swatting on Days 1 through 6?

3. If she swatted 288 in the first hour, 312 the second hour, and 336 the third hour, how many will she swat in the fourth hour?

4. Louise rested from her swatting 3 minutes in one hour. In the next hour, she rested 6 minutes. In the fourth hour she rested 24 minutes. How long will she rest in the fifth hour?

5. On Monday, Louise swatted mosquitoes for ten hours. Finish the pattern for her swats for hours 1 through 10.

   820, 780, _____, 700, 660, _____, _____, _____, _____, _____

6. On Tuesday, Louise swatted 125 the first hour, 150 the second hour, 200 the third hour, 300 the fourth hour and 500 the fifth hour. What is the pattern?

Name _____

LONG-DISTANCE CRICKET SPITTING

Yes! People spit crickets for fun and sport! At a three-day insect celebration during the annual Bug Bowl, competitors see who can spit dead crickets the farthest. The record belongs to Danny Caps. He actually spit a cricket 32 feet, $\frac{1}{2}$ inch.

Look at the Cricket-Spitting Records table.
Notice that some numbers are missing.
Figure out the pattern in each row.
Write the numbers to finish the pattern.

CRICKET-SPITTING DATA

Competitor's Name	Distance in Feet
Lance	22
Fran	16
Sam	11
Van	25
Stan	31
Pam	21
Nan	18

CRICKET-SPITTING RECORDS

Competitor and Pattern	1st Try	2nd Try	3rd Try	4th Try	5th Try	6th Try
Lance (add 3)						22
Fran (multiply by 2)	1					32
Sam (subtract 2)			37			
Vance (multiply by 1)			25			
Stan (add 3, then 4, then 5, and so on)	3					
Pam (add 2 twice, add 3 three times)	8					
Nan (subtract 1, 2, 3, and so on)	18					

Name _____

Common Core Reinforcement Activities — 4th Grade Math

SPORTS TRIVIA

Find and follow the pattern to solve these problems with fun sports facts.

1. Yuki's weight of 412 pounds is average for a sumo wrestler. Then, he loses 15 pounds in January, 30 in February, and 45 in March. How much will he weigh at the end of May?

_____

2. The heaviest weight lifted in Olympic competition weighed 262.5 kilograms. During practice, one weightlifter lifted 120 kg on Monday, 130 on Tuesday, 141 on Wednesday, and 153 on Thursday. How much weight did he lift on Saturday?

_____

3. The first game of basketball as we know it was played in 1892 with two peach basket hoops. Finish the pattern by filling in the missing numbers.

473 _____ 1,892 3,784 _____

What is the pattern? _____

4. A balance beam used in competition is 10 centimeters wide. Finish the pattern by filling in the missing number.

20,000   2,000   200 _____ 2

What is the pattern? _____

5. Eight-ball is a popular game played on a pool table. The game is played with 7 solid color balls, 7 striped balls, a white cue ball, and the black 8 ball. Amanda collected striped pool balls. Finish the pattern by filling in the missing number to find the total number she collected.

7   15   31   63   127   ____

Mmmm

6. On average, a golf ball has 400 dimples. Finish the pattern by filling in the missing number.

20,000   4,000   800 _____ 32

What is the pattern?_____

7. In a hockey game, when one player scores 3 goals in one game, it is said that she or he has accomplished a "hat trick." In season 1, Pam's team had 4 hat tricks. In season 2, there were 7 hat tricks. In season 3, there were 10 hat tricks. How many hat tricks would you expect in season 4?

_____

8. There are 3,000 meters in a cross country race. To train, Lucus ran several miles a week. Here is his mileage for the past seven weeks. Follow the pattern to find the missing mileage for weeks 5 and 7.

60   68   70   78   ____   88   ____

Name

NUMBER
AND
OPERATIONS
IN
BASE TEN

Grade 4

ATHLETES ON PARADE

The Olympic Games begin with a parade of athletes who will compete in the Games. In 2008 thousands of athletes competed in the Summer Olympics in Bejing, China, for 17 days. Hundreds of medals were given, thousands of visitors attended, and three billion more watched on TV. In 2010, it started all over again when thousands of athletes traveled to Vancouver, British Columbia, Canada for the Winter Olympics.

Solve these problems about some numbers that match Olympic facts.

1. Eleven thousand twenty-eight athletes competed in Bejing.

   Write this as a numeral: _____

2. The Bejing Olympics cost forty-three billion dollars.

   Write this as a numeral: _____

3. 958 medals were given at the Bejing Olympics.

   How many ones are represented by the 5 in this number? _____

4. 2,583 special lights were used as a part of the opening Olympic ceremony in Bejing.

   How many tens are represented by the 5 in this number? _____

5. 4,300,000,000 people around the world watched the Bejing Olympics on TV.

   Write this number in words: _____

6. 70,070 people attended the closing ceremony at the 2004 Summer Olympics in Athens, Greece. Compare this number to another number.

   Write > or < in the box.   **70,070** ☐ **70,707**

7. The TV rights for the 1992 Barcelona Summer Olympic Games were sold for $40,100,000.

   How many ten thousands are represented by the 1 in this number? _____

8. Twenty-nine thousand, two hundred, twenty-eight athletes participated in the 1988, 1992, and 1996 Summer Olympic Games combined.

   Write the numeral for this number: _____

Use with page 37.

Name _____

36

Solve these problems about some numbers that match Olympic facts.

9. Three billion people watched the 2010 Vancouver Olympics on TV.

   Write this as a numeral: _____

10. 2,566 athletes competed in the 2010 Games in Vancouver.

    How many hundreds are represented by the 2 in this number? _____

11. In Vancouver, 258 medals were awarded.

    How many ones are represented by the 5 in this number? _____

12. A total of 7,473 athletes competed in the 2002, 2006, and 2010 Olympics combined.

    How many ones are represented by the 4 in this number? _____

13. 147 nations took part in the 2012 Paralympic Games in London.

    How many ones are represented by this number? _____

14. 10,000 workers from media companies came to the 2010 Vancouver Winter Olympic Games.

    How many thousands are represented by this number? _____

15. Sixty-one thousand, six hundred people attended the opening ceremony at the Vancouver Games. Write this number on the blank line. Compare it to the other number by writing > or < in the box.

    _____ ☐ **6,100,000**

16. At the 1996 Summer Olympics in Atlanta, Georgia, athletes won a total of 1,933 medals.

    Write this number in words. _____

17. One million, three hundred thousand tickets were available for the 1998 Winter Olympics. Write this number on the blank line. Compare it to the other number by writing > or < in the box.

    _____ ☐ **1,030,300**

18. In the 2012 London, England Summer Olympics, 205 nations participated in 300 events. What is the difference in the number of hundreds in these two numbers (205 and 300)?

    _____

Use with page 36.

Name _____

A BIG RACE—A WARM POOL

At the 2012 Summer Olympics in London, the Aquatic Center had seats for 17,500 people to watch swimming and diving events. The three pools held 10 million liters of water, and the cost was about 242 million Euros.

There are many numbers around Olympic Games—numbers of people, medals, scores, distances, measurements, and amounts of money!

Read these numbers written in words.
Write the numerals into the puzzle to match the clues.

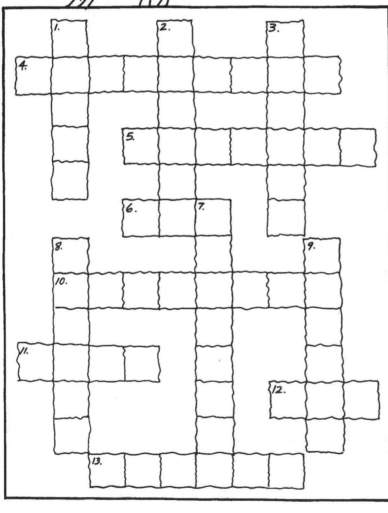

DOWN

1. forty thousand, nine hundred, seventy-three
2. one hundred fifty-one thousand, six hundred
3. nine hundred thousand, nine hundred, one
7. seventy-one million, eight hundred thousand, three
8. six hundred ten thousand, three hundred, ninety
9. four hundred fifty thousand, nine

ACROSS

4. three hundred million, fifty thousand, eight
5. two million, six hundred thousand, nine hundred
6. two hundred seven
10. twelve million, eight thousand, thirty-five
11. eight thousand, three hundred, fifty-one
12. nine hundred nine
13. three hundred thousand, three hundred

Name

SNATCH, CLEAN, AND JERK

Snatch, clean, and *jerk* may not sound like sports words—but they are! These strange words tell the names of the important moves in weightlifting. To perform a snatch, the lifter brings the weight from a platform to an overhead hold in one movement. To perform a clean and jerk, the lifter pulls more weight, but the lift has two parts. First, the lifter brings the weight to his shoulders, and then he or she lifts it overhead.

1. Look at these weights lifted by some Olympic athletes. Read the numbers, and put them in order by numbering from 1 to 12 to show the numbers from smallest to largest, with 1 being the smallest.

_____	Alexandre	462 kg
_____	Leonid	425 kg
_____	Manfred	430 kg
_____	Martin	407 kg
_____	Dean	412 kg
_____	Mario	410 kg
_____	Sulton	440 kg
_____	Jurgen	411 kg
_____	Todeuz	408 kg
_____	Vassili	441 kg
_____	Helmut	387 kg
_____	Rudolf	610 kg

2. Number these from smallest to largest.

_____	72,999
_____	70,859
_____	107,200
_____	17,040
_____	5,966
_____	1,000,000
_____	600,000
_____	51,030
_____	999,999

— Olympic Fact —

Tommy Kono was sick as a child. His parents tried to cure his asthma with powdered snakes, burned bird, and bear kidneys. During World War II, his family was sent to a Japanese-American detention camp. It was a terrible time for his family, but he was introduced to weightlifting there. Tommy won a gold medal as a weightlifter in 1952.

Name _____

HIGH SPEEDS AND TOUGH TURNS

The Super Giant Slalom is said to take the most skill of any ski event. Skiers race down a mountain over a long, steep course at speeds of up to 80 miles per hour. They must go through a series of gates marked by flags.

Write a number from one of the flags that includes each value. The first one is done for you.

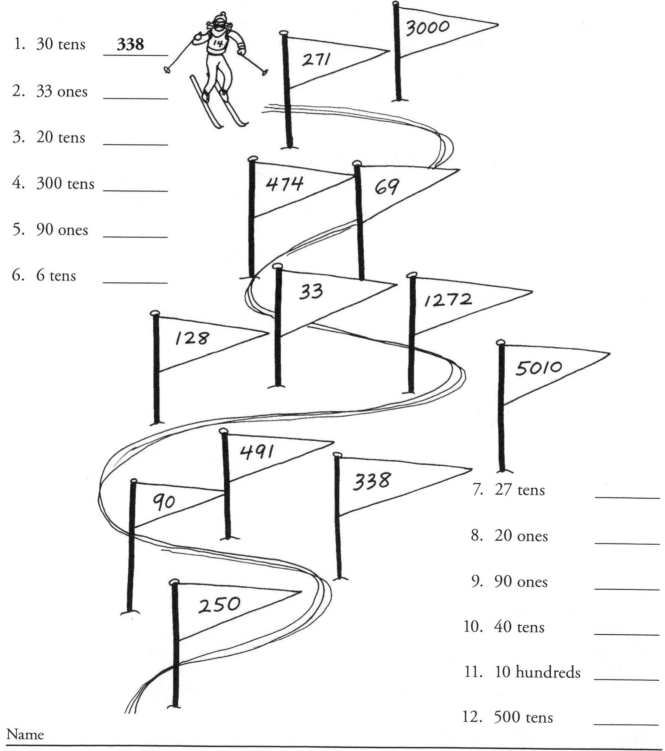

1. 30 tens   **338**

2. 33 ones   _____

3. 20 tens   _____

4. 300 tens   _____

5. 90 ones   _____

6. 6 tens   _____

7. 27 tens   _____

8. 20 ones   _____

9. 90 ones   _____

10. 40 tens   _____

11. 10 hundreds   _____

12. 500 tens   _____

Name

WHAT'S THE VALUE?

In this sport, the right equipment is of great value! Identify this important equipment as you focus on place value. Follow the clues to color each puzzle space. Look for a number with the value described.

Blue
1. six tens
2. 22 hundreds
3. eight ones
4. 10 tens
5. 72 thousands
6. 900 tens
7. 80 ones
8. 4500 tens
9. sixty tens
10. 11 tens, 2 ones
11. 70 tens
12. 48 ones

Red
13. 120 hundreds
14. 70 ones

White
15. nine ones
16. 20 thousands
17. one 10, four ones
18. four ones
19. three ones

Yellow
20. five tens
21. 60 hundreds

Purple
22. 80 tens
23. 800 tens
24. six ones
25. 70 thousands
26. two tens
27. 30 tens
28. 17 tens
29. 1 ten, six ones

Orange
30. 12 hundreds
31. 48 hundreds

Green
All spaces with other numbers

Name

Common Core Reinforcement Activities — 4th Grade Math

THE ETERNAL FLAME

In the 2012 Summer Olympic Games, 10,500 athletes gathered under the Olympic flag to compete in 302 events in 26 different sports. They represented 204 different countries. The most breathtaking Olympic symbol was the Olympic Torch. Its flame came from a torch that burns constantly in Athens, Greece. Every Olympic year, the flame is carried to the host city by a torch relay that includes many people.

When Olympic information is reported, numbers are often rounded for easier reporting. Round each of these numbers to the digit that is underlined.

1. 10,750 _____

2. 271 _____

3. 1,933 _____

4. 357 _____

5. 891 _____

6. 7,486 _____

7. 15,426 _____

8. 4,542 _____

9. 800,426 _____

10. 754,086 _____

11. 999,999 _____

12. 101,326 _____

13. 60,600 _____

14. 774,688 _____

15. 10,987 _____

16. 766 _____

17. 98,922 _____

18. 609 _____

19. 555 _____

20. 55,555 _____

21. 923 _____

22. 18,533 _____

23. 600,001 _____

24. 1,507 _____

Name _____

CLEAN JUMPS, PLEASE!

Show jumping is one of the most thrilling and most televised of all the Olympic equestrian events. The rider takes the horse around a course full of obstacles at top speeds. On the way, the rider tries to keep control of the horse and to avoid trips, falls, or other faults!

Help this rider get around this course without errors. Round each number to the place that is underlined. Write the answer on each obstacle the horse must jump.

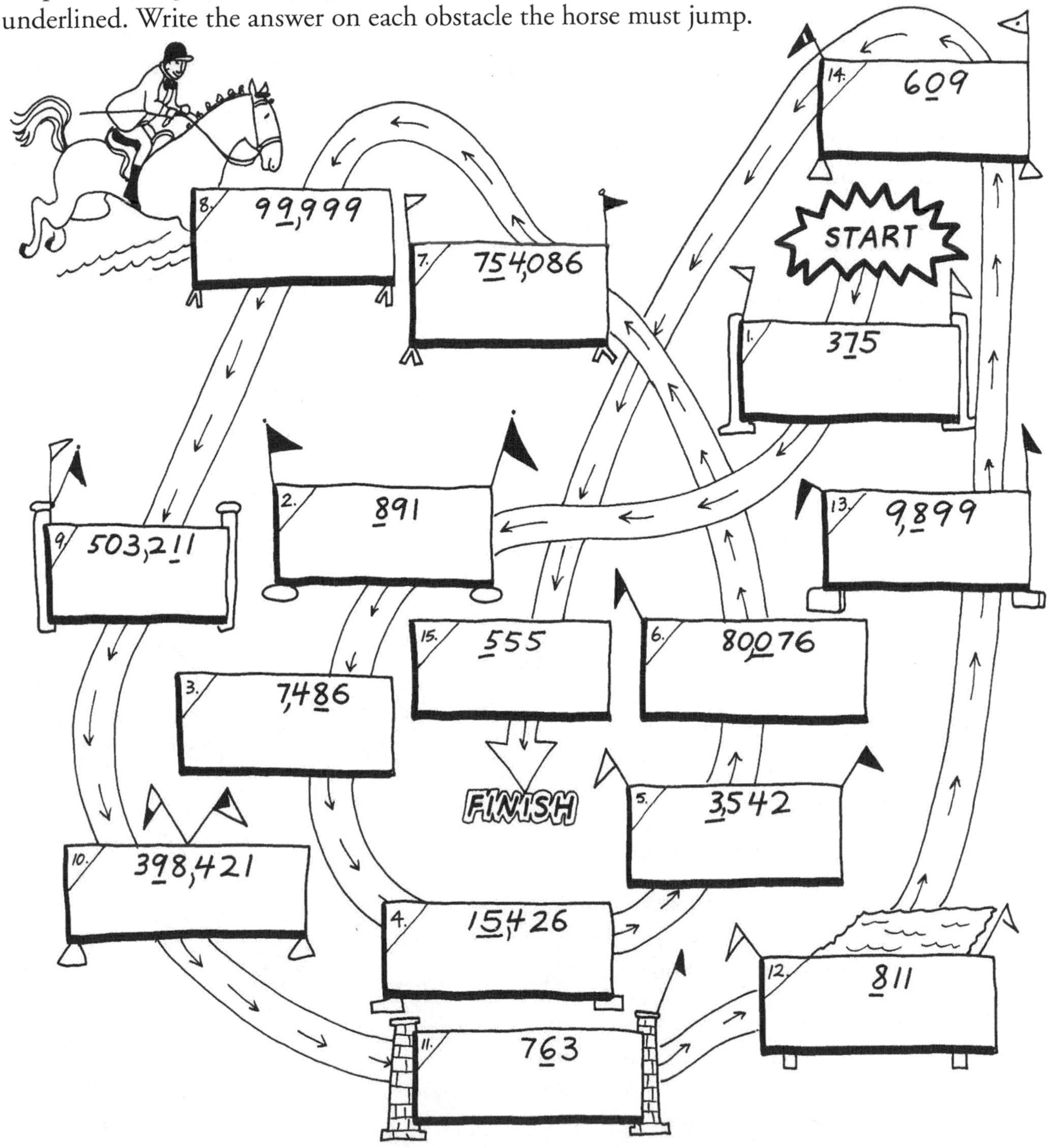

14. 6_0_9

START

8. 9_9_,999

7. 75_4_,086

1. 3_7_5

9. 503,2_1_1

2. _8_91

13. 9,_8_99

15. _5_55

6. 80_0_76

3. 7,4_8_6

5. 3,_5_42

10. 39_8_,421

4. 15_4_26

12. _8_11

11. 7_6_3

FINISH

HOLD YOUR BREATH

In the sport of synchronized swimming, swimmers spend 60% of the routine under the water. They do difficult, synchronized movements while holding their breaths. And they are not allowed to touch the bottom or side of the pool!

Follow the instructions to round some numbers about Olympic swimming.

> **─ Olympic Fact ─**
> Synchronized swimming used to be called water ballet. The U.S. team won the gold in this event at the 1996 Olympics.

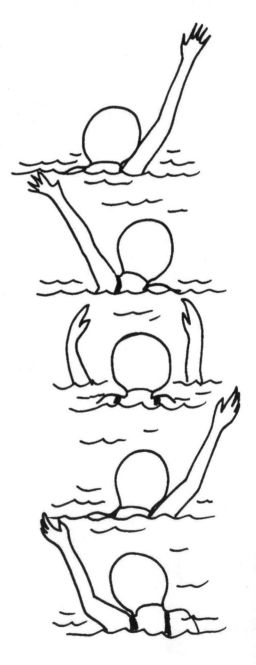

1. Synchronized swimming became an official Olympic sport in the 1984 Summer Olympic Games. Round this number to the nearest hundred: _____

2. In 2008, China won the bronze medal in the team synchronized swimming event. The technical score was 48,584. Round this number to the nearest ten: _____

3. At the Olympics, a team synchronized swimming routine cannot last more than 255 seconds. Round this number to the nearest ten: _____

4. Most synchronized swimmers can swim 75 meters and hold their breath for three minutes Round this number to the nearest ten: _____

5. To hear the music underwater, the swimmers need special speakers. These cost about $2,500 each. Round this number to the nearest thousand: _____

6. A duet team of synchronized swimmers practiced 1,149 hours in a year. Round this number to the nearest hundred: _____

7. An Olympic-sized swimming pool holds 660,430 gallons of water. Round this number to the nearest ten thousand: _____

8. The Aquatic Center for the 2012 Olympic Games in London, England, is said to have cost 303,000,000 euros. Round this number to the nearest hundred million: _____

Name _____

THE BIG WINNERS

TOP 30 MEDAL WINNERS OLYMPIC SUMMER GAMES 1896 - 2008

Country	Medals
USA	4335
USSR/Russia	2687
United Kingdom	1594
France	1314
Italy	1228
Germany	1211
Australia	1075
Hungary	1053
Sweden	1021
Netherlands	782
Japan	708
China	679
Romania	624
Canada	592
Norway	537
Poland	499
Denmark	491
South Korea	466
Finland	451
Yugoslavia	435
Belgium	408
Czechoslovakia/ Czech Republic/ Slovakia	399
Cuba	395
Spain	377
Switzerland	376
Brazil	372
Bulgaria	331
Argentina	239
India	178
New Zealand	164

The modern Olympic Games began in 1896. Since then, thousands of gold, silver, and bronze medals have been awarded to hard-working athletes A new design for medals is created for each Olympic Games.

Use the medal-counts on the table to solve the problems. Do your work on a separate piece of paper.

1. The total medals won by the top 5 countries equals _____ .

2. Norway's medals plus Canada's medals equal _____ .

3. _____ won 816 more medals than Cuba.

4. The United Kingdom won _____ fewer medals than the USA.

5. _____ won 469 fewer medals than Japan.

6. Russia/USSR and Czechoslovakia/Czech Republic/ Slovakia together won _____ medals.

7. The Netherlands won _____ fewer than Hungary.

8. Romania won 248 more medals than _____ .

9. Before the 2008 Olympics, Spain had a total of 360 medals. How many did Spain win in 2008? _____

10. Before the 2008 Olympics, Brazil had a total of 357 medals. How many did Brazil win in 2008? _____

Name _____

KNOCK OUT!

Boxing was not allowed at the first modern Olympics in 1896 because it was considered too ungentlemanly and dangerous. Today it is a very popular Olympic sport. Some of the world's greatest boxers, such as Floyd Patterson, Muhammad Ali, Sugar Ray Leonard, Joe Frazier, Leon Spinks, and Evander Holyfield, won Olympic medals before becoming professional boxers.

See if you can knock out these subtraction problems by getting all the answers right!

1.
```
   500
 − 229
```

2.
```
   900
 − 683
```

3.
```
    40
 −  26
```

4.
```
   300
 − 258
```

5.
```
   407
 − 133
```

6.
```
    90
 −  55
```

7.
```
   800
 − 393
```

8.
```
  5500
 −  203
```

9.
```
  9050
 − 5348
```

10.
```
  7001
 − 6420
```

11.
```
  6110
 −  456
```

12.
```
  8006
 −  731
```

13.
```
  800,321
 − 79,001
```

14.
```
  32,000
 − 19,862
```

— Olympic Fact —

One of the most memorable moments of the 1996 Summer Olympic Games in Atlanta was when boxing legend and 1960 gold medal-winner Muhammad Ali (who suffers from Parkinson's disease) lit the Olympic torch.

Name

EN GARDE!

Fencing was an event at the first modern Olympic Games in 1896. It is an old sport that began around 400 B.C. Fencers use different kinds of swords: the foil, the épée, and the sabre. When the bout director calls "en garde," the competitors take a ready position. They begin the bout when the director gives the command: "fence."

Try your skill in this bout with addition and subtraction.

1.
$$47 + 9$$

2.
$$234 + 78$$

3.
$$864 - 342$$

4.
$$179 + 761$$

5.
$$89 + 24$$

6.
$$333 - 222$$

7.
$$712 + 542$$

8.
$$666 - 477$$

9.
$$973 - 458$$

10.
$$229 + 644$$

11.
$$30,068 + 95,581$$

12.
$$8149 + 2889$$

13.
$$8000 - 505$$

14.
$$6161 - 4099$$

15.
$$10,000 - 7108$$

16.
$$7400 - 42$$

épée = 770 grams

Sabre = 500 grams

foil = 500 grams

Olympic Fact

Fencers began to wear white uniforms because ink from the end of the weapon would leave a spot when a hit was made. The ink showed up well on the white. This practice is no longer followed, but fencers still wear the white uniforms. Some fencers would dip their uniforms in vinegar so the mark would not show.

Name

MAKING IT OVER THE HURDLES

The Olympic hurdle event is a fast sprinting race with a series of barriers to jump. The hurdles are mostly made of metal, and sometimes runners knock them over as they jump. It doesn't disqualify a hurdler to knock one over, but usually it slows him or her down a little. Men and women compete in hurdle events of different lengths and with different height hurdles.

Help this runner clear her hurdles by solving the problems correctly. Start with the first number, and do all the operations shown to find the final answer.

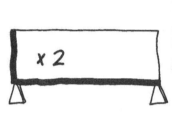
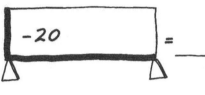

Solve these problems the same way.

1. **(20 x 4)** + 100 – 10 = _____

2. **(50 x 10)** + 500 ÷ 2 = _____

3. **777 – 555 + 333 + 444 =** _____

4. **(888 ÷ 4)** x 3 + 111 + 100 = _____

5. **(1 + 15 + 14)** x 2 = _____

6. **(200 x 10)** – 100 + 9 + 90 = _____

7. **(4,200 ÷ 2)** – 100 + 30 = _____

8. **(1,000 x 5)** + 5,000 – (10 x 100) = _____

— Olympic Fact —

In 1988, hurdler Gail Devers faced the biggest hurdle of her life. Due to Grave's disease, she could not walk. Doctors thought they would have to amputate her feet. Instead, she came back to win gold medals in the 100-meter sprint at the 1992 and 1996 Olympics.

Name _____

THE RIGHT STUFF

Hockey players need the right equipment to play the game safely. They also need the right skills and a good understanding of the rules. Show that you have the right skills and understanding to solve these multiplication problems.

Finish the calculations to show how multiplication works for each problem. The first two are completed for you.

1.   1,224
          x   3

3 x 1,000 =   3,000
3 x 200 =   600
3 x 20 =   60
3 x 4 =   +   12

                 3,672

2.   22
          x 23

20 x 20 =   400
20 x 2 =   40
3 x 20 =   60
3 x 2 =   +   6

                  506

3.   15
          x 45

40 x 10 =   400
40 x 5 =   200
5 x 10 =   50
5 x 5 =   +   25

4.   8,034
          x   5

5 x 8,000 = _____
5 x 0 =   _____
5 x 30 =   _____
5 x 4 =   + _____

5.   558
          x   6

6 x 500 = _____
6 x 50 =   _____
6 x 8 = + _____

6.   82
          x   36

30 x 80 = _____
30 x 2 =   _____
6 x 80 =   _____
6 x 2 = + _____

7.   6,543
          x   3

3 x 6,000 = _____
3 x 500 =   _____
3 x 40 =   _____
3 x 3 =   + _____

8.   974
          x   4

4 x 900 = _____
4 x 70 =   _____
4 x 4 = + _____

9.   69
          x   18

10 x 60 = _____
10 x 9 =   _____
8 x 60 =   _____
8 x 9 = + _____

Name _____

Common Core Reinforcement Activities — 4th Grade Math

MAY THE BEST SAILOR WIN

Yachting has been an Olympic sport since the 1896 games in Athens. Unfortunately, the yachting races had to be canceled at those games! The weather was just too bad. In each racing class, all the yachts must have the same design. This way, the best sailor wins the race, not the best boat!

Solve the multiplication problems in the puzzle. Use the color code to find the color for each section. If you get the answers right, the colored picture will show you one kind of yacht used in Olympic racing.

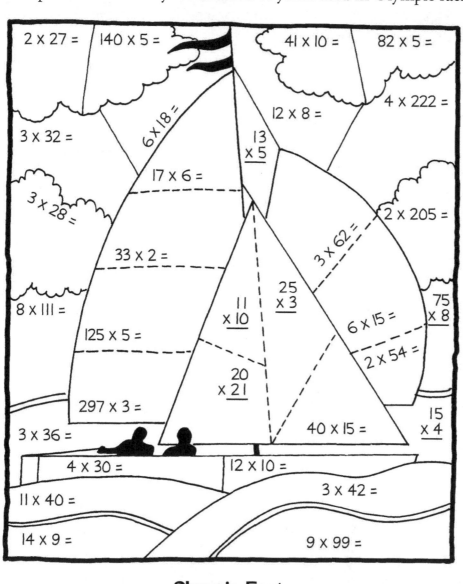

COLOR CODE

| **Red** |
| 66, 186 |

| **Hot Pink** |
| 54, 84, 410, 700 |

| **Purple** |
| 102, 420 |

| **White** |
| 625, 75 |

| **Dark Blue** |
| 440, 60, 891, 110 |

| **Bright Green** |
| 65, 90, 108, 126 |

| **Brown** |
| 120 |

| **Yellow** |
| 108, 888 |

| **Orange** |
| 96, 600 |

Puzzle problems:
2 x 27 =   140 x 5 =   41 x 10 =   82 x 5 =
6 x 18 =   12 x 8 =   4 x 222 =
3 x 32 =   13 x 5 =
17 x 6 =
3 x 28 =
2 x 205 =
33 x 2 =   3 x 62 =
8 x 111 =   11 x 10 =   25 x 3 =   6 x 15 =   75 x 8 =
125 x 5 =   2 x 54 =
20 x 21 =
297 x 3 =
40 x 15 =   15 x 4 =
3 x 36 =
4 x 30 =   12 x 10 =
3 x 42 =
11 x 40 =
14 x 9 =   9 x 99 =

— Olympic Fact —

Competitors sail one race each day of the competition. The crew throws out its worst race. All the other scores are added together. The lowest score wins!

Name

50

SAILING WITHOUT A SAIL

It's spectacular . . . breathtaking . . . awesome! Crowds at the Winter Olympics always love to watch the ski jumpers sailing through the air. Spectators hold their breath until the skier lands safely on the ground! Skiers gain points for strong take-offs, smooth flights, clean landings, and distance. Skiers take off into the air from jumps as high as 120 meters and sail for hundreds of meters.

Use multiplication to figure out these distances.

1. 23 meters x 10 = _____

2. 23 meters x 100 = _____

3. 31 meters x 30 = _____

4. 111 meters x 1,000 = _____

5. 505 meters x 10 = _____

6. 2,222 meters x 400 = _____

7. 717 meters x 10,000 = _____

8. 4,024 meters x 20 = _____

9. 70 meters x 40 = _____

10. 250 meters x 1,000 = _____

Use division to figure out these distances.

11. 4,400 meters ÷ 10 = _____

12. 4,400 meters ÷ 100 = _____

13. 4,400 meters ÷ 200 = _____

14. 1,000 meters ÷ 10 = _____

15. 1,000 meters ÷ 100 = _____

16. 330 meters ÷ 10 = _____

17. 880,000 meters ÷ 1,000 = _____

18. 700 meters ÷ 70 = _____

19. 5,600 meters ÷ 80 = _____

20. 61,070 meters ÷ 10 = _____

— Olympic Fact —

Judges stand at one-meter intervals along the edge of the hill and watch to see where the ski jumpers land.

They decide the distances with their eyes instead of measuring with any tools.

Name _____

Common Core Reinforcement Activities — 4th Grade Math

TOURIST ATTRACTIONS

Two million people attended the 2012 Summer Olympic Games. They bought tickets, watched events, traveled around the London area, stayed in hotels or homes, and bought lots of food and souvenirs. (The money used in London is *pounds*. The symbol for this is £.)

Use your division skills to solve each of these problems about Olympic visitors.

1. One family bought 8 full-price tickets for the kayaking finals. They paid a total of £760. How much did each ticket cost? _____

2. Assume that sausages sold for £4 in the Olympic Village, and that a total of £6,500,000 was taken in for sausages. How many sausages were sold? _____

3. Bus drivers in London demanded a bonus for driving during the Olympic Games in 2012. The cost of their bonus would total £4000 for 8 drivers. How much was the bonus request for each driver? _____

4. One family drove 654 kilometers from their home to London for the Olympic Games. They drove for 6 hours. How many kilometers did they average per hour? _____

5. The best seats for the diving finals at the London Summer Games cost £450. Antonio's dad bought the tickets, but Antonio paid for one-fifth of his own. How much did Antonio pay? _____

6. Another family drove 1,308 kilometers to London for the Summer Olympic Games. They drove for 12 hours. What was the average number of kilometers per hour? _____

7. Britta's family bought 9 Olympic basketballs as souvenirs to take home to friends. The total cost was £252. What was the cost of each basketball? _____

8. A group of six friends earned £900 to buy tickets to the Opening Ceremony of the 2012 Olympic Games for themselves. What was the cost for each ticket? _____

Name

FANS BY THE THOUSANDS

Each country that hosts Olympic Games spends a lot of money and many years getting ready. Some countries use sports arenas that they already have. But most countries build a new Olympic Stadium. The stadium built in Atlanta, Georgia, in 1996 held 85,000 fans.

If the 85,000 seats in the stadium were arranged in 50 equal sections, you could divide to find the number of seats in each section. Use division to solve these problems about the number of seats in sections of different arenas.

1. Aquatic Center—swim events   14,000 seats ÷ 20 sections = _____

2. Georgia World Congress—fencing, judo   7,500 seats ÷ 25 sections = _____

3. Georgia Tech Coliseum—boxing   9,500 seats ÷ 10 sections = _____

4. Nagano's Hockey Arena—hockey   10,000 seats ÷ 50 sections = _____

5. White Ring—speed skating   7,300 seats ÷   5 sections = _____

6. Nagano Olympic Stadium   50,000 seats ÷ 50 sections = _____

7. Atlanta Olympic Stadium   85,000 seats ÷ 50 sections = _____

8. Clark University Stadium—field hockey   5,000 seats ÷ 25 sections = _____

9. Georgia Dome—basketball   32,000 seats ÷   8 sections = _____

10. Omni Coliseum—baseball   52,000 seats ÷ 40 sections = _____

11. $9\overline{)8190}$ 12. $3\overline{)1227}$ 13. $6\overline{)9534}$ 14. $8\overline{)46,328}$

Olympic Fact

Atlanta spent $500 million on new buildings for the 1996 Olympics.

The Olympic Stadium cost $209 million.

CRISS-CROSS BIKE RACE

In this bicycle race, each cyclist will follow a different path. The four paths will cross each other many times. Start with the circle by Biker #1, using a red crayon or marker. Color the circle red.

Using mental math, do the operation shown on the flag. Draw a red line to the circle that has that answer. Color it red. Do the next operation and keep drawing the path until you reach a trophy.

Use green for #2, blue for #3, and purple for #4 to draw paths for the other bikers.

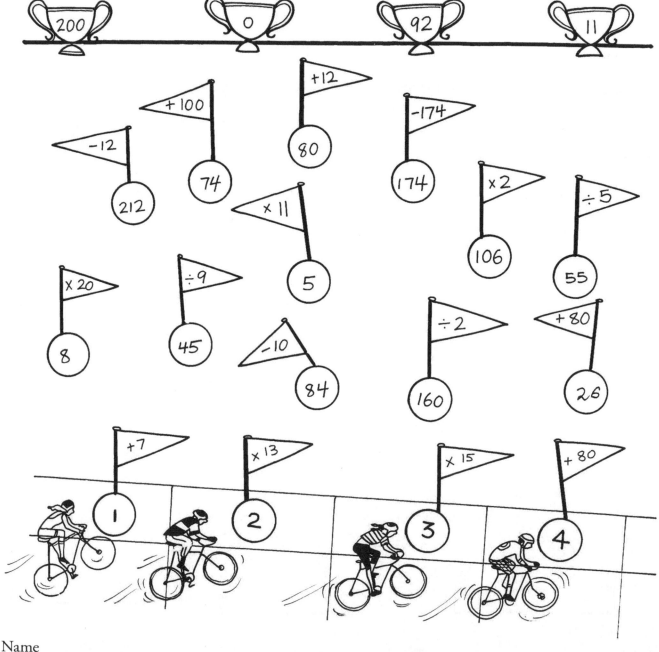

NUMBER
AND
OPERATIONS—
FRACTIONS

Grade 4

Ya hoo !

WATCH THAT PUCK!

Olympic Fact
The 1998 Winter Olympics in Japan were the first Games that permitted women to compete in ice hockey.

These fans are gathered for an exciting hockey game. All the game is focused on that little rubber disc. The puck moves so fast that it is hard to tell which team has it. At the 1980 Olympics, USA fans were very excited when the team beat Finland to win its first gold medal in 20 years.

Pay attention to these fans to practice your skills with equivalent fractions. Write your answers in the blanks.

1. $\frac{2}{6}$ of the fans are holding balloons. Explain why this fraction is equivalent to $\frac{1}{3}$.

   _____

2. $\frac{6}{9}$ of the flags have no words. Explain why this fraction is equivalent to $\frac{2}{3}$.

   _____

3. $\frac{4}{12}$ of the feet have on boots. Explain why this fraction is equivalent to $\frac{2}{6}$.

   _____

4. $\frac{2}{8}$ of the cups have two straws. Explain why this fraction is equivalent to $\frac{1}{4}$.

   _____

5. Black is the color on $\frac{1}{9}$ of the flags.

   Write an equivalent fraction: _____

6. $\frac{4}{6}$ of the fans are wearing hats.

   Write an equivalent fraction: _____

7. $\frac{4}{10}$ of the balloons are held by the girl with pigtails.

   Write an equivalent fraction: _____

8. $\frac{12}{12}$ of the hands are covered with gloves or mittens.

   Write an equivalent fraction: _____

9. $\frac{2}{5}$ of the shoes or boots have laces.

   Write an equivalent fraction: _____

10. There is no straw in $\frac{1}{8}$ of the cups.

   Write an equivalent fraction: _____

Name _____

WINTER OLYMPIC TRIVIA

Learn some interesting Olympic facts as you identify equivalent fractions!

In each problem, two fractions are equivalent to one another.
Find the one that is NOT. Circle it.

That one will be beside the answer to the trivia question.

1. Luge sleds can reach speeds over

   $\frac{16}{18}$ 80 mph

   $\frac{8}{9}$ 300 mph

   $\frac{5}{9}$ 140 mph

2. The oldest game played on ice is

   $\frac{2}{3}$ curling

   $\frac{1}{5}$ ice hockey

   $\frac{6}{9}$ ice bowling

3. Downhill racers travel at speeds of over

   $\frac{4}{5}$ 200 mph

   $\frac{7}{9}$ 130 mph

   $\frac{12}{15}$ 80 mph

4. The number of competitors riding each luge sled is

   $\frac{3}{5}$ 1 or 2

   $\frac{4}{7}$ 3 or 4

   $\frac{8}{14}$ 4 or 5

5. The first Olympics that included snowboarding was in

   $\frac{1}{3}$ 1992

   $\frac{7}{21}$ 1984

   $\frac{5}{8}$ 1998

6. The speedskating rink in Lillehammer in 1994 was shaped like a

   $\frac{7}{8}$ ice skate

   $\frac{9}{12}$ Viking ship

   $\frac{28}{32}$ snowshoe

7. People have been using skis for

   $\frac{1}{11}$ 9,000 years

   $\frac{2}{12}$ 200 years

   $\frac{1}{6}$ 100 years

8. The ski jumping record is

   $\frac{3}{4}$ about 800 feet

   $\frac{6}{7}$ about 1 mile

   $\frac{18}{21}$ about 2,000 feet

9. The biathlon combines

   $\frac{1}{2}$ skating and skiing

   $\frac{5}{11}$ cross-country skiing and rifle shooting

   $\frac{2}{4}$ luge and bobsled

10. The most difficult ice skating jump landed in Olympic competition (as of 2010) was

   $\frac{1}{4}$ triple lutz

   $\frac{2}{8}$ triple axle

   $\frac{2}{6}$ quadruple salchow

Name

Common Core Reinforcement Activities — 4th Grade Math

OVER THE NET

Beach volleyball began in the 1940s on the beaches of California. It was played for fun at first, but now it is a serious professional sport. It did not gain a place at the Olympic Games until 1996, when the U.S. men's teams won the gold and silver medals.

Write each pair of fractions as new fractions with a common denominator. Compare the two fractions. Insert <, >, or = between the two fractions.

Olympic Fact

In beach volleyball, each team has only two players.

They play barefoot in the sand.

1. $\frac{2}{4}$ $\frac{3}{5}$ 2. $\frac{4}{6}$ $\frac{1}{3}$ 3. $\frac{4}{8}$ $\frac{2}{4}$

4. $\frac{2}{7}$ $\frac{1}{3}$

5. $\frac{1}{3}$ $\frac{1}{6}$

6. $\frac{5}{6}$ $\frac{1}{3}$

7. $\frac{3}{4}$ $\frac{7}{8}$ 8. $\frac{2}{5}$ $\frac{4}{10}$

9. $\frac{5}{8}$ $\frac{2}{3}$ 10. $\frac{7}{9}$ $\frac{11}{12}$ 11. $\frac{2}{10}$ $\frac{5}{6}$ 12. $\frac{1}{5}$ $\frac{2}{10}$

Rewrite the fractions in order from smallest to largest.

13. $\frac{1}{2}$ $\frac{2}{5}$ $\frac{1}{4}$ 14. $\frac{3}{18}$ $\frac{5}{6}$ $\frac{2}{3}$ 15. $\frac{2}{5}$ $\frac{6}{8}$ $\frac{5}{10}$

_____   _____   _____

Name _____

LOST!

Badminton may look like an easy sport where you just hit the "birdie" around at a slow pace. Actually, it is the world's fastest racket sport. The "birdies" are called *shuttlecocks*, and they travel as fast as 200 miles per hour!

On the way to the competition, Pierre got separated from his badminton team. To help him join his teammates, compare the fractions in each box. Color any box that has a correct sign (>, <, or =). If you do this correctly, you will color a path for Pierre to his teammates.

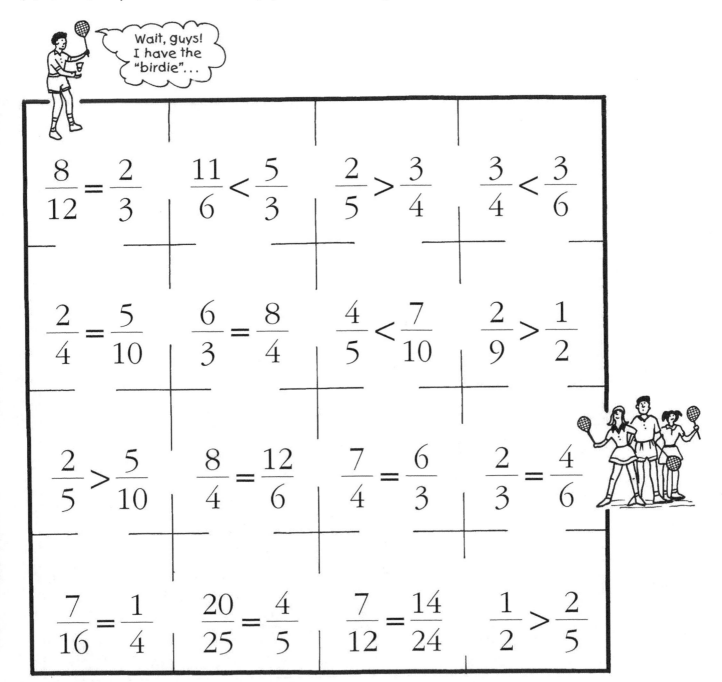

$\dfrac{8}{12} = \dfrac{2}{3}$	$\dfrac{11}{6} < \dfrac{5}{3}$	$\dfrac{2}{5} > \dfrac{3}{4}$	$\dfrac{3}{4} < \dfrac{3}{6}$
$\dfrac{2}{4} = \dfrac{5}{10}$	$\dfrac{6}{3} = \dfrac{8}{4}$	$\dfrac{4}{5} < \dfrac{7}{10}$	$\dfrac{2}{9} > \dfrac{1}{2}$
$\dfrac{2}{5} > \dfrac{5}{10}$	$\dfrac{8}{4} = \dfrac{12}{6}$	$\dfrac{7}{4} = \dfrac{6}{3}$	$\dfrac{2}{3} = \dfrac{4}{6}$
$\dfrac{7}{16} = \dfrac{1}{4}$	$\dfrac{20}{25} = \dfrac{4}{5}$	$\dfrac{7}{12} = \dfrac{14}{24}$	$\dfrac{1}{2} > \dfrac{2}{5}$

Name

Common Core Reinforcement Activities — 4th Grade Math

THE #1 SPORT

Soccer is the most popular sport in the world. (In most places it is called *football*.) It was the first team sport to be included in the Olympics. At every Olympic Games, this sport draws some of the biggest crowds. In 1992, at the Barcelona, Spain Games, the mainly Spanish crowd was thrilled to see their team win the gold medal!

Look on the soccer field below for the answer to each problem. Circle the correct answer with the color shown. Then write it on the line. Answers must be fractions in lowest terms.

Example: $\frac{1}{10} + \frac{1}{2} = \frac{1}{10} + \frac{5}{10} = \frac{6}{10}$ ($\frac{3}{5}$ *in lowest terms*)

1. GREEN: $\frac{2}{3} + \frac{1}{6} =$ _____

2. RED: $\frac{5}{10} - \frac{1}{5} =$ _____

3. BLUE: $\frac{5}{12} - \frac{1}{3} =$ _____

4. YELLOW: $\frac{3}{4} - \frac{5}{8} =$ _____

5. PURPLE: $\frac{1}{4} + \frac{4}{16} =$ _____

6. BROWN: $\frac{10}{25} + \frac{2}{5} =$ _____

7. ORANGE: $\frac{11}{12} - \frac{3}{4} =$ _____

8. PINK: $\frac{1}{2} + \frac{2}{22} =$ _____

9. RED: $\frac{20}{30} - \frac{2}{6} =$ _____

10. BLUE: $\frac{1}{9} + \frac{2}{3} - \frac{1}{3} =$ _____

11. PURPLE: $\frac{2}{9} + \frac{8}{9} - \frac{1}{3} =$ _____

12. GREEN: $\frac{4}{7} + \frac{1}{3} =$ _____

13. ORANGE: $\frac{11}{14} - \frac{3}{7} + \frac{1}{7} =$ _____

14. BROWN: $\frac{1}{6} + \frac{3}{4} - \frac{1}{8} =$ _____

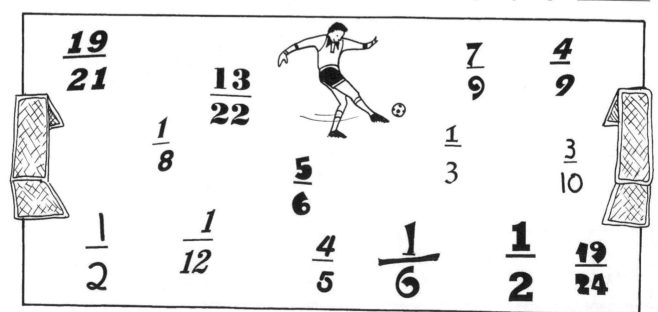

Name

PENTATHLON CALCULATIONS

Penta means *five*, and athlon means *competition*. So athletes who compete in the pentathlon must be good at five different sports. The modern pentathlon includes five events: pistol shooting, fencing, 200 m freestyle swimming, show jumping, and a 3 km cross-country run.

Each of these calculations has five parts. You'll need to be skilled at each step in order to finish with the right answer. Write all answers in lowest terms.

1. $\frac{9}{10} - \frac{1}{10} + \frac{7}{10} + \frac{5}{10} - \frac{1}{10} =$ _____

2. $\frac{7}{9} - \frac{3}{9} - \frac{2}{9} + \frac{6}{9} - \frac{2}{9} =$ _____

3. $\frac{2}{13} + \frac{5}{13} - \frac{4}{13} + \frac{10}{13} - \frac{6}{13} =$ _____

4. $\frac{5}{6} - \frac{2}{6} + \frac{6}{6} - \frac{2}{6} - \frac{3}{6} =$ _____

5. $\frac{3}{20} - \frac{1}{20} + \frac{15}{20} - \frac{4}{20} + \frac{2}{20} =$ _____

6. $\frac{1}{11} + \frac{5}{11} + \frac{8}{11} - \frac{9}{11} + \frac{1}{11} =$ _____

7. $\frac{1}{5} - \frac{1}{5} + \frac{2}{5} + \frac{9}{5} - \frac{6}{5} =$ _____

8. $\frac{4}{16} - \frac{2}{16} + \frac{7}{16} + \frac{5}{16} + \frac{1}{16} =$ _____

9. $\frac{5}{25} - \frac{3}{25} + \frac{9}{25} - \frac{2}{25} + \frac{1}{25} =$ _____

10. $\frac{6}{12} - \frac{5}{12} + \frac{7}{12} - \frac{7}{12} + \frac{1}{12} =$ _____

11. $\frac{9}{6} - \frac{2}{6} + \frac{10}{6} - \frac{3}{6} + \frac{15}{6} =$ _____

12. $\frac{11}{100} + \frac{15}{100} - \frac{4}{100} + \frac{50}{100} - \frac{1}{100} =$ _____

Name _____

Common Core Reinforcement Activities — 4th Grade Math

FROSTY SPORTS

Most sports at the Winter Olympics are outdoor sports. Even if the competitions are held indoors, the temperatures are usually cold to keep the ice from melting. You'll need to be good with fractions to solve these puzzles with facts about the Winter Olympics.

QUESTION: *Which event has brought the most Winter Olympic medals to the U.S.?*

1. Write the second $\frac{1}{6}$ of SKIING. _____ **K** _____

2. Write the first $\frac{1}{4}$ of ATTITUDE. _____

3. Write the first $\frac{1}{3}$ of SPECTATOR. _____

4. Write the first $\frac{1}{4}$ of GOLD. _____

5. Write the last $\frac{1}{5}$ of SNOWBOARDS. _____

6. Write the first $\frac{1}{10}$ of ICE DANCING. _____

7. Write the last $\frac{1}{4}$ of GAME. _____

8. Write the last $\frac{1}{8}$ of BIATHLON. _____

ANSWER: *Unscramble the letters to find the sport of*

_____

Olympic Fact

Olympic gold medal winner Dan Jansen has skated over 100,000 miles on his speed skates.

This is more than 4 times the distance around the world.

QUESTION: *In which ski event did USA skier Lindsey Vonn win a gold medal at the 2010 Winter Olympics?*

1. Write the first $\frac{1}{6}$ of NAGANO. _____

2. Write the first $\frac{1}{4}$ of LUGE. _____

3. Write the second $\frac{1}{5}$ of SNOWBOARDS. _____

4. Write the second $\frac{1}{8}$ of OLYMPICS. _____

5. Write the third $\frac{1}{5}$ of MEDAL. _____

6. Write the first $\frac{1}{5}$ of HIGHLIGHTS. _____

ANSWER: *Unscramble the letters to find this event:*

_____

Name _____

THE LONGEST JUMPS

It sounds pretty hard! An athlete runs down a short path and jumps as far as possible, landing into a pit of sand. A measurement is taken from the beginning of the jump to the impression the body leaves in the sand. If the athlete falls backward from where the feet land, the measurement will be shorter than desired!

— Olympic Fact —

U.S. track and field athlete Jackie Joyner-Kersee won the gold medal in 1988 with a jump of 24 ft $3\frac{1}{2}$ in.

U.S. jumper Carl Lewis won the gold medal in the long jump at four Olympic Games: 1984, 1988, 1992, & 1996.

Here are some measurements of long jumps from athletes of all ages. They are written as improper fractions. Write them as mixed numerals in lowest terms.

1. Carlos $\frac{12}{2}$ ft + $\frac{45}{2}$ ft = _____ ft = _____ ft

2. Lutz $\frac{26}{6}$ ft + $\frac{33}{6}$ ft = _____ ft = _____ ft

3. Shakira $\frac{10}{4}$ ft + $\frac{87}{4}$ ft = _____ ft = _____ ft

4. Heide $\frac{27}{2}$ ft + $\frac{20}{2}$ ft = _____ ft = _____ ft

5. Andrea $\frac{15}{5}$ ft + $\frac{17}{5}$ ft = _____ ft = _____ ft

6. Yvette $\frac{26}{8}$ ft + $\frac{61}{8}$ ft = _____ ft = _____ ft

7. Julio $\frac{55}{3}$ ft + $\frac{33}{3}$ ft = _____ ft = _____ ft

8. Ari $\frac{66}{4}$ ft − $\frac{17}{4}$ ft = _____ ft = _____ ft

9. Randall $\frac{116}{4}$ ft − $\frac{7}{4}$ ft = _____ ft = _____ ft

10. Tatiana $\frac{96}{3}$ ft − $\frac{25}{3}$ ft = _____ ft = _____ ft

11. Marita $\frac{100}{5}$ ft − $\frac{27}{5}$ ft = _____ ft = _____ ft

12. Roberto $\frac{120}{5}$ ft + $\frac{45}{5}$ ft = _____ ft = _____ ft

Name

Common Core Reinforcement Activities — 4th Grade Math

WHEN IS A SHELL A SCULL?

Rowing is an exciting Olympic sport. Boats used for competitive rowing are called *shells*. Some of the shells are *sculls*. In a scull, each crew member rows with two oars instead of one. The boats are very light and move quickly over the 2,000-meter course.

Solve each row of problems as quickly as the crews row the shells. Don't be sloppy, or it will take longer to correct your mistakes! Can you tell which boat is the scull? Write answers in lowest terms.

1. $5\frac{3}{8} + 6\frac{3}{8} =$ _____

2. $17\frac{2}{8} + 9\frac{3}{8} =$ _____

3. $22\frac{4}{5} - 5\frac{2}{5} =$ _____

4. $15\frac{2}{4} - 5\frac{1}{4} =$ _____

9. $7\frac{2}{5} - 6\frac{1}{5} =$ _____

10. $30\frac{3}{11} - 20\frac{2}{11} =$ _____

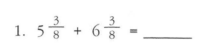

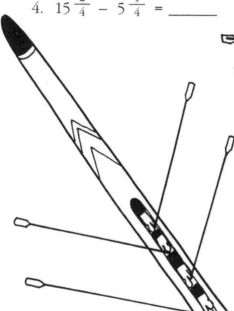

5. $10\frac{1}{4} + 1\frac{3}{4} =$ _____

6. $8\frac{1}{5} - 5\frac{1}{5} =$ _____

7. $5\frac{2}{3} + 5\frac{1}{3} =$ _____

8. $18\frac{1}{6} - 8\frac{1}{6} =$ _____

11. $2\frac{3}{9} + 4\frac{1}{9} =$ _____

12. $16\frac{2}{5} + 3\frac{2}{5} =$ _____

13. $32\frac{1}{5} - 7\frac{1}{5} =$ _____

14. $20\frac{1}{6} - 5 =$ _____

15. $\frac{1}{10} + 5\frac{9}{10} =$ _____

Name

GOAL OR NOT?

Some scoring attempts in soccer end up being only attempts! Other attempts result in a goal. Read the graph to find out how many of the attempts by the Bay City soccer players were successful.

Solve the problems. Replace one or both of the fractions with equivalent fractions with the same denominators. Write answers in lowest terms.

1. Tess goals scored in relation to attempts: $\frac{9}{12}$
   plus
   Dana goals scored in relation to attempts: $\frac{4}{16}$
   $$\frac{9}{12} + \frac{4}{16} = \frac{3}{4} + \frac{1}{4} = \underline{\hspace{1cm}}$$

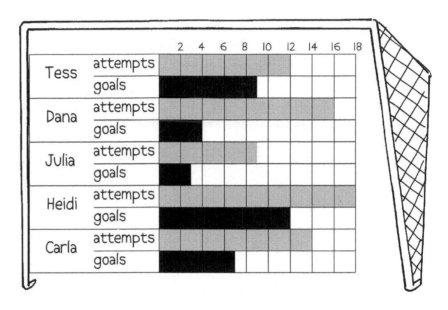

		2	4	6	8	10	12	14	16	18
Tess	attempts									
	goals									
Dana	attempts									
	goals									
Julia	attempts									
	goals									
Heidi	attempts									
	goals									
Carla	attempts									
	goals									

2. Julia plus Heidi
   $$\frac{3}{9} + \frac{12}{18} = \frac{1}{3} + \frac{2}{3} = \underline{\hspace{1cm}}$$

3. Carla plus Tess
   $$\frac{7}{14} + \frac{9}{12} = \frac{1}{2} + \frac{3}{4} =$$
   $$\frac{2}{4} + \frac{3}{4} = \underline{\hspace{1cm}}$$

4. Heidi minus Dana $\quad \frac{12}{18} - \frac{4}{16} = \frac{2}{3} - \frac{1}{4} = \frac{8}{12} - \frac{3}{12} = \underline{\hspace{1cm}}$

5. Tess minus Julia $\quad \frac{9}{12} - \frac{3}{9} = \frac{3}{4} - \frac{1}{3} = \frac{9}{12} - \frac{4}{12} = \underline{\hspace{1cm}}$

6. Dana plus Heidi $\quad \frac{4}{16} + \frac{12}{18} = \frac{1}{4} + \frac{2}{3} = \frac{3}{12} + \frac{8}{12} = \underline{\hspace{1cm}}$

Solve the problems. Replace each mixed number with an equivalent fraction. Write answers in lowest terms.

7. $1\frac{3}{5} + 8\frac{1}{5}$ $\underline{\hspace{1.5cm}}$

8. $9\frac{3}{10} - 5\frac{4}{10}$ $\underline{\hspace{1.5cm}}$

9. $20\frac{1}{4} - 9\frac{3}{4}$ $\underline{\hspace{1.5cm}}$

10. $12\frac{2}{3} + 10\frac{1}{3}$ $\underline{\hspace{1.5cm}}$

Name

Common Core Reinforcement Activities — 4th Grade Math

TUGGING PROBLEMS

Take a close look at the team members in this tug-of-war game. You'll need to pay attention to the clothes they are wearing in order to solve the problems.

Write an equation to solve each problem. The equation will be an addition or subtraction problem with two fractional numbers. Write the answer in lowest terms.

1. Find the fraction of the group that is wearing hats. Find the fraction of the group that is wearing shirts. What is the total of these amounts? _____

2. Find the fraction of the feet that have black shoes or boots. Find the fraction of the feet that have black socks. What is the difference between these two amounts? _____

3. Draw bandages on $\frac{7}{20}$ of the total number of knees. Then, solve this problem: What fraction represents the number of knees without bandages?

_____

4. What fraction of the group is wearing neither a hat nor striped pants?

$1 - \underline{\hspace{1cm}} - \underline{\hspace{1cm}} = \underline{\hspace{1cm}}$

5. Draw bruises on 9 elbows. Then solve this problem: What fraction of the total elbows have bruises? _____

6. Color 3 of the shirts blue. Color 4 of the shirts red. What fraction represents the number of shirts that are neither blue nor red?

$1 - \underline{\hspace{1cm}} - \underline{\hspace{1cm}} = \underline{\hspace{1cm}}$

7. $\frac{2}{5}$ of the whole group (both teams) got stung by bees. Five other group members ran away. What fraction of the original number was left—that did not get stung and did not run away?

$1 - \underline{\hspace{1cm}} - \underline{\hspace{1cm}} = \underline{\hspace{1cm}}$

Name

BRUNO'S BURLY BREW

Big Bruno makes energy shakes for all his weight-lifting friends. One batch makes enough for four weightlifters. Solve the problems related to Bruno's recipe. Write an equation for each problem. Write answers in lowest terms.

1. Bruno decided to add $1\frac{2}{3}$ cups of milk to his brew. How much milk was then in the shake? _____

2. By mistake, Bruno put in $\frac{6}{4}$ teaspoons of vanilla. How much extra vanilla ended up in the shake? _____

3. Bruno decided to double the amount of protein powder in this batch. How much protein powder ended up in the shake? _____

4. Just for fun, Bruno also added an additional $3\frac{1}{2}$ bananas to the shake. How many bananas ended up in the shake? _____

5. Bruno shared this shake with 2 other friends. He gave $\frac{1}{5}$ of the shake to the first friend, $\frac{2}{5}$ of the shake to the second friend. How much was left for him? _____

6. In the next shake, Bruno will use $\frac{3}{4}$ cup less of milk. How much milk will be in that shake? _____

3 cups of milk
6 raw eggs
$2\frac{1}{2}$ bananas
$\frac{3}{4}$ teaspoon vanilla
$\frac{2}{3}$ cup of protein powder

Name _____

Copyright © 2014 World Book, Inc./
Incentive Publications, Chicago, IL

SKATING QUESTIONS

Sonja Henie was eleven years old when she entered her first Olympic Games in 1924. Even though this young figure skater finished last, she did not give up. She came back three more times and won the gold medal every time! She was known for her interesting, graceful movements and her fancy costumes.

Skaters need plenty of practice. Practice your fraction skills to answer these skating questions.

1. A skater spent $\frac{1}{7}$ of her performance spinning and $\frac{3}{7}$ of her performance jumping. What part of the performance was spent doing other moves?

   a. $\frac{4}{7}$ b. $\frac{4}{14}$ c. $\frac{3}{7}$

2. Kristina spent $\frac{1}{10}$ of her skating budget on skates, $\frac{3}{10}$ of it on costumes, and the rest on traveling and training. What fraction of the budget was spent on traveling and training?

   a. $\frac{4}{10}$ b. $\frac{3}{5}$ c. $\frac{6}{20}$

3. Sergi spends four-sixths of his practice time on technical moves such as spins and jumps. He spends the rest working on artistic moves. How much time does he spend on artistic moves?

   a. $\frac{1}{3}$ b. $\frac{2}{3}$ c. $\frac{6}{10}$

4. Miranda placed first in $\frac{5}{12}$ of the competitions she entered. She placed third in $\frac{1}{12}$ of them. She placed second in the rest. In what fraction of the competitions did she place second?

   a. $\frac{1}{2}$ b. $\frac{6}{24}$ c. $\frac{7}{12}$

5. Rudolph spends $\frac{1}{6}$ of each year training in Germany and the rest of the year training in Switzerland. What fraction of the year does he spend in Switzerland?

   a. $\frac{6}{6}$ b. $\frac{5}{6}$ c. $\frac{5}{12}$

6. Natasha's coach always pays for $\frac{4}{5}$ of the cost of hot drinks for her on practice mornings. What fraction of the cost is left for Natasha to pay?

   a. $\frac{2}{10}$ b. $\frac{1}{5}$ c. $\frac{5}{5}$

7. Louisa has been ice skating for $\frac{9}{15}$ of her life. For $\frac{3}{15}$ of her life, she was a roller skater. Before that, she did not skate at all. What fraction of her life did she not skate?

   a. $\frac{12}{15}$ b. $\frac{3}{5}$ c. $\frac{1}{5}$

Name

HITTING THEIR STRIDE

To skate their fastest time, speed skaters need to "hit their stride." This means they need to get their steps (strides) moving in the right rhythm that keeps them moving fast.

Check the accuracy of these math statements. If a statement is correct, color the matching section of the speed skating track.

1. Skating time of $\frac{3}{4}$ hour = 75 minutes.

2. $\frac{6}{7}$ mile + $1\frac{2}{7}$ miles = $2\frac{1}{7}$ miles.

3. $\frac{8}{12}$ is equivalent to $\frac{2}{3}$.

4. $\frac{3}{4}$, $\frac{18}{24}$, and $\frac{6}{8}$ are all equivalent.

5. $\frac{5}{9}$ mile + $\frac{2}{9}$ mile = $\frac{7}{18}$ mile.

6. $\frac{12}{20}$ hour − $\frac{7}{20}$ hour = $\frac{5}{10}$ hour.

7. $4\frac{1}{8}$ + $4\frac{4}{8}$ − $3\frac{5}{8}$ = $11\frac{1}{8}$

8. $\frac{30}{40}$ is equivalent to $\frac{6}{8}$.

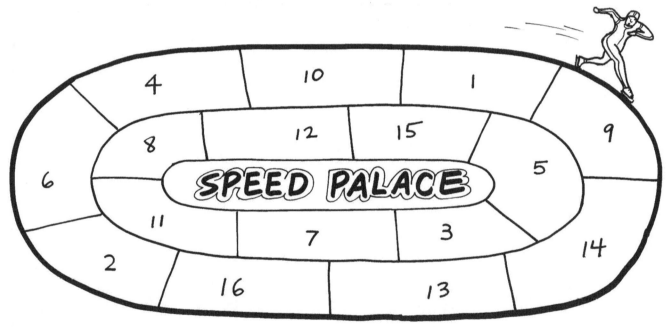

9. $\frac{5}{50}$ of a race's distance, $\frac{1}{10}$ of that race, and $\frac{15}{150}$ of that race all represent the same distance.

10. $\frac{18}{22}$ − $\frac{5}{22}$ + $\frac{4}{22}$ + $\frac{3}{22}$ = $\frac{10}{11}$

11. A skating time of $5\frac{1}{2}$ minutes is the same as $\frac{12}{2}$ minutes.

12. The difference between $10\frac{5}{7}$ and $4\frac{6}{7}$ is $4\frac{1}{7}$.

13. $\frac{1}{6}$ + $\frac{3}{6}$ of a 1,000-meter race = 400 meters.

14. This group of fractions is written smallest to greatest: $\frac{2}{5}$; $\frac{1}{3}$; $\frac{4}{9}$.

15. Three skaters each ate $1\frac{2}{3}$ pounds of pasta. The sum of all the pasta they ate was 5 pounds.

Name

Common Core Reinforcement Activities — 4th Grade Math

BE CAREFUL NOT TO SWING

A male gymnast does some difficult moves while he hangs from rings. Gymnasts show amazing skill and strength as they hold their bodies in hard positions. The rings are not supposed to swing or wobble. The gymnast's body and arms are not supposed to wobble, sag, or shake.

Keep these rings from wobbling by identifying the multiples. Follow the directions to color some of the rings.

1. Color multiples of $\frac{1}{7}$: RED.
2. Color multiples of $\frac{2}{9}$: BLUE.
3. Color multiples of $\frac{1}{8}$: GREEN.
4. Color multiples of $\frac{2}{15}$: YELLOW.

5. Color multiples of $\frac{4}{22}$: PURPLE.
6. Color multiples of $\frac{1}{20}$: ORANGE.
7. Color multiples of $\frac{3}{12}$: PINK.
8. Color multiples of $\frac{4}{25}$: BROWN.

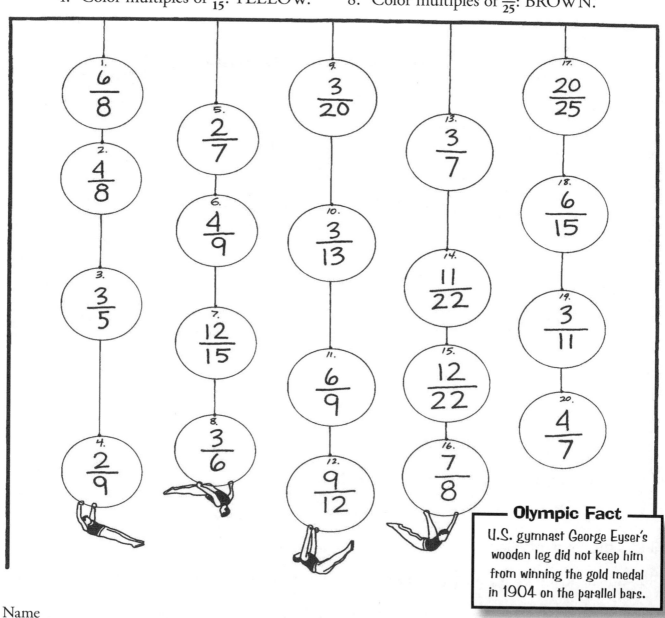

Olympic Fact

U.S. gymnast George Eyser's wooden leg did not keep him from winning the gold medal in 1904 on the parallel bars.

Name

THROUGH WILD WATERS

In the Olympic kayaking events, kayakers race through wild, foaming water (known as whitewater). They must get down the river through a series of gates safely and speedily. Some of the gates require them to paddle upstream against the raging waters! Of course, sometimes the kayaks flip, but the athletes are good at turning right side up again.

Answer each question *yes* or *no* to show your understanding of multiples.

_____ 1. Is $\frac{5}{6}$ a multiple of $\frac{3}{6}$?

_____ 2. Is $\frac{3}{3}$ a multiple of $\frac{4}{6}$?

_____ 3. Is $\frac{12}{4}$ a multiple of $\frac{3}{4}$?

_____ 4. Is $\frac{12}{18}$ a multiple of $\frac{4}{18}$?

_____ 5. Is $\frac{7}{6}$ a multiple of $\frac{3}{6}$?

_____ 6. Is $\frac{10}{8}$ a multiple of $\frac{2}{8}$?

_____ 7. Is $\frac{13}{21}$ a multiple of $\frac{13}{7}$?

_____ 8. Is $\frac{5}{15}$ a multiple of $\frac{10}{15}$?

_____ 9. Is $\frac{4}{7}$ a multiple of $\frac{1}{7}$?

_____ 10. Is $\frac{10}{15}$ a multiple of $\frac{5}{15}$?

_____ 11. Is $\frac{8}{20}$ a multiple of $\frac{2}{20}$?

_____ 12. Is $\frac{39}{5}$ a multiple of $\frac{13}{5}$?

Name _____

HOT OLYMPIC STEW

Forty-eight cold, hungry skiers planned to stop at the ski lodge to warm up with some hearty Olympic Stew. The cook's recipe was intended to serve twenty-four, so she knew she'd have to double the recipe to have enough.

Rewrite the stew recipe for 48. Use your fraction multiplication skills to get the right amounts. Write the new fractions in lowest terms.

Olympic Stew for 24

$5\frac{1}{2}$ pounds potatoes
$8\frac{1}{4}$ quarts boiling water
2 large onions
$8\frac{1}{8}$ cups chicken broth
$4\frac{2}{3}$ carrots, chopped
$8\frac{1}{2}$ celery sticks, sliced
$1\frac{1}{2}$ green peppers, chopped
$5\frac{1}{3}$ cups frozen corn
$4\frac{3}{4}$ pounds mushrooms
$7\frac{1}{4}$ cups cooked chicken, diced
$3\frac{1}{3}$ teaspoons salt
$6\frac{1}{3}$ Tablespoons mixed herbs
Mix all ingredients in a large pot. Cook over medium heat for one hour, stirring often.

Olympic Stew for 48

_____
_____
_____
_____
_____
_____
_____
_____
_____
_____
_____
_____
_____
_____

Name

HANG THOSE TOES!

The surf's up at Shark Beach! One hundred surfers showed up on Saturday to "hang ten" for the awesome waves. Hanging ten is special stunt where the surfer positions the board so that the wave is at the back of the board and he or she can hang all ten toes over the nose of the surfboard.

Choose a fraction from the waves that will solve each of the multiplication problems.

1. $11 \times \frac{2}{10} =$ _____

2. $5 \times \frac{2}{22} =$ _____

3. $2 \times \frac{7}{7} =$ _____

4. $3 \times \frac{4}{30} =$ _____

5. $4 \times \frac{1}{3} =$ _____

6. $\frac{2}{15} \times 3 =$ _____

7. $7 \times \frac{3}{5} =$ _____

8. $3 \times \frac{3}{11} =$ _____

9. $\frac{5}{25} \times 2 =$ _____

10. $\frac{2}{10} \times 4 =$ _____

11. $\frac{5}{100} \times 3 =$ _____

12. $2 \times \frac{3}{14} =$ _____

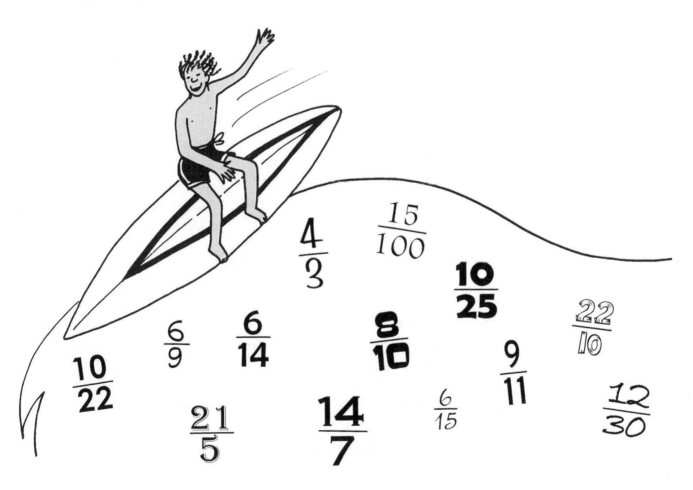

Name _____

Common Core Reinforcement Activities — 4th Grade Math

TIME OUT

The Cramville basketball team is crammed into their bus, headed for the big game. On the way to Eagletown, the Cramville Comets have some unexpected stops.

Solve these problems about their trip. Write the answers in lowest terms.

_____ 1. The team left Cramville at 8:00 A.M. They drove $22\frac{3}{4}$ miles the first hour and 3 times that far in the second hour. How far did they drive from 9:00 to 10:00 A.M.?

_____ 2. They stopped 4 times for gas. Each stop took $15\frac{3}{8}$ minutes. How long did they spend stopped at gas stations?

_____ 3. They hit a terrible rainstorm that stopped them for $\frac{3}{4}$ hour and after that, they were stuck in the mud for twice that long. How long were they stuck in the mud?

_____ 4. Ooops! After the mud problems, they had four flat tires. It took $3\frac{2}{3}$ minutes to change each one. How long did it take to change all four?

_____ 5. The bus stopped for a snack break. The driver said, "You have 35 minutes." But everyone was back in the bus in $\frac{1}{5}$ that time. How long did the break take?

_____ 6. The bus came upon three different accidents. Each one delayed the trip by $2\frac{5}{6}$ hours. How long were they delayed by accidents?

_____ 7. Once again, the bus was stopped! This time, a herd of 15 cows blocked the road. It took $2\frac{1}{4}$ minutes for each cow to get out of the way. How long did they wait for the cows?

_____ 8. After the cow problem, the bus engine sputtered to a stop. So Coach got on the phone and ordered pizza. Each of the 21 team members ate $\frac{3}{12}$ of a pizza. Coach ate the same amount. How much pizza did they eat?

Name _____

"BUT COACH, CAN WE REST NOW?"

What are the coaches cooking up now? They are probably trying to figure out how to keep their players working, improving, and winning. Here are some of the challenges the coaches are facing.

Help them solve the problems. Write the answers in lowest terms.

_____ 1. Of the 20 players on Coach Jasmin's basketball team, only $\frac{1}{5}$ are good at dunking the ball. How many are good dunkers?

_____ 2. Roberto swam $\frac{3}{5}$ of the 120 laps that Coach Samantha asked him to do. How many laps did he swim?

_____ 3. Coach Strikeout ordered 24 new ball caps for his team. Only $\frac{1}{4}$ arrived on time. How many did not arrive?

_____ 4. Coach Swift watched 12 of his runners finish a $6\frac{3}{4}$ mile run. What was the total of their mileage?

_____ 5. Coach Leap's team has only one hurdler. Unfortunately, she knocks over about $\frac{5}{8}$ of the 24 hurdles every time she runs. How many hurdles does she knock down?

_____ 6. Coach Puck's hockey team keeps losing the hockey pucks! Last week, Coach bought 36 new pucks. The team lost $\frac{6}{9}$ of the pucks. How many were lost?

_____ 7. When Coach Lobb's volleyball team went into the locker room, they threw $\frac{9}{10}$ of the 40 towels on the floor. How many towels were on the floor?

_____ 8. By the end of the ski season, $\frac{5}{6}$ of Coach Mogul's 30 skiers had been injured. How many were injured?

Name _____

FANTASTIC FINISHES

Solve these problems about the race and the runners.

1. Each of these runners ran $\frac{7}{8}$ of a mile during the race.
    What was the total of their distances? _____

Find the missing number.

2. Before the race, Michael did 12 different stretches—each one for $\frac{1}{2}$ a minute. How many minutes did he stretch?

    $12 \times \frac{1}{2} = n$ n = _____

3. During a 10-mile race, Alberto stopped 7 times to rest. Each time, he rested for $\frac{1}{3}$ of a minute. How many minutes did he rest?

    $\frac{1}{3} \times 7 = n$ n = _____

4. Jojo practiced by running $\frac{8}{10}$ of a mile twice a day for 30 days. How many miles did he run in practice?

    $\frac{8}{10} \times 60 = n$ n = _____

5. Leah drinks $\frac{2}{5}$ liter of water each hour on the day of the race. She did this for 6 hours before the race. How many liters did she drink?

    $\frac{2}{5} \times 6 = n$ n = _____

6. After a race, 6 runners shared pizzas. Each ate $\frac{3}{4}$ of a pizza. Use the number line to represent what they ate. Use a different color arrow to show what each ate.

    What total amount of pizza did they eat? _____

Name _____

OVER THE TOP

Pole vaulters sprint along a short track with a long pole that bends easily. Then they plant the pole into sand and soar upside down over a bar that might be as high as 20 feet. The goal is to make it over the top without knocking off that bar!

If a pole vaulter makes it over the bar 35 times out of a hundred, the success rate can be shown with a fraction: $\frac{35}{100}$ (which means 35 hundredths). This fraction means the same as $\frac{3}{10}$ plus $\frac{5}{100}$ because $\frac{3}{10}$ is equivalent to $\frac{30}{100}$.

BOING

Express each fraction that has a denominator of ten as an equivalent fraction with a denominator of 100. Then add the fractions.

Athlete	Problem		Success Rate
1. Maxim	$\frac{6}{10} + \frac{4}{100} =$	$\frac{60}{100} + \frac{4}{100} =$	$\frac{64}{100}$
2. Javier	$\frac{8}{10} + \frac{9}{100} =$	$\frac{80}{100} + \frac{9}{100} =$	_____
3. Angela	$\frac{7}{10} + \frac{3}{100} =$	_____ + _____ =	_____
4. Philippa	$\frac{4}{10} + \frac{8}{100} =$	_____ + _____ =	_____
5. Will	$\frac{9}{10} + \frac{0}{100} =$	_____ + _____ =	_____
6. Gregory	$\frac{5}{10} + \frac{2}{100} =$	_____ + _____ =	_____
7. Katya	$\frac{7}{10} + \frac{7}{100} =$	_____ + _____ =	_____
8. Brie	$\frac{6}{10} + \frac{6}{100} =$	_____ + _____ =	_____

Name _____

Common Core Reinforcement Activities — 4th Grade Math

THE DREAM TEAM

No one doubted that the United States Olympic basketball team would win a gold medal in Barcelona in 1992. This team had the world's best professional players, including Magic Johnson and Michael Jordan. The players were high scorers. They had great success with free throws.

The table shows the rate of free throw success for each of the players. Write each fraction as a decimal numeral.

FREE THROW RATES FOR CHAMPIONSHIP GAME

Player	Fraction	Decimal	Player	Fraction	Decimal
Magic	$\frac{85}{100}$		Karl	$\frac{59}{100}$	
Christian	$\frac{63}{100}$		Patrick	$\frac{63}{100}$	
Clyde	$\frac{83}{100}$		Larry	$\frac{75}{100}$	
David	$\frac{54}{100}$		John	$\frac{50}{100}$	
Charles	$\frac{85}{100}$		Chris	$\frac{64}{100}$	
Michael	$\frac{75}{100}$		Scottie	$\frac{68}{100}$	

1. Which player's rate was lower than David's? _____

2. How many players had a rate higher than Clyde? _____

3. Which players had the same rate of success? _____

    _____

4. Which player had a rate of sixty-eight hundredths? _____

5. Which player had a rate ten hundredths higher than David's? _____

6. What was the difference between Karl's rate and Clyde's rate? _____

Name _____

TAKE THE PLUNGE

Imagine jumping off a three-story building into a pool of water! That is what platform divers do. Olympic divers begin at a standstill and jump off a high platform, or they jump off a bouncy springboard. Seven judges watch each dive and score it between 1 and 10. Scores for 11 dives are added together. The diver with the highest score wins. At the 2000 Summer Games in Sydney, Australia, American Laura Wilkinson won the gold medal in platform diving with a score of 370.71.

Find a decimal in the pool to match each of the decimal words below.

1. seventy-five hundredths _____

2. seven and five tenths _____

3. fifty-five hundredths _____

4. five hundred and five hundredths _____

5. seventy-five _____

6. ninety hundredths _____

7. five hundredths _____

8. nine and nine tenths _____

9. five and seven hundredths _____

10. fifty-five and five tenths _____

11. nine and ninety-nine hundredths _____

12. eleven and six tenths _____

13. one and sixteen hundredths _____

14. sixteen hundredths _____

0.75   0.55   **0.16**   9.99

7.5   500.05   **5.07**

11.6   0.05   **0.90**   75

55.5   1.16   9.9

Name

Common Core Reinforcement Activities — 4th Grade Math

NOSE ROLLS AND FAKIES

This must be the sport with the wildest names for moves and tricks! On a snowboard you can do Halfpipes, Nose Rolls, Wheelies, McTwists, Chicken Salads, and Ollies—-and many more tricks with wild, wacky names! 1998 was the first time snowboarders could take part in the Olympic Games. The boarders were ready to do all these fancy tricks, and more, in Japan!

To finish each of these tricks with a good score, read the decimals on each card. Then number them in order from the smallest to the largest.

Trick #1 FAKIE

____	0.11103	____	1.7
____	0.103	____	11.3
____	10.37	____	13.01
____	11.370	____	0.13

Trick # 5 CHICKEN SALAD

____	2.6	____	6.2
____	2.7	____	2.9
____	2.06	____	22.6
____	26.6	____	2.999

Trick #2 NOSE ROLL

____	15.02	____	15.21
____	1.5	____	1.51
____	0.005	____	55.5
____	0.05	____	5.5

Trick #3 BACKSCRATCHER

____	4.5	____	4.7
____	0.451	____	44.5
____	0.45	____	4.4
____	0.06	____	0.44

Trick #6 OLLIE

____	7.2	____	7.7
____	0.72	____	77.27
____	0.072	____	0.07
____	72.1	____	0.007

Trick #4 McTWIST

____	5.28	____	5.6
____	9.97	____	0.009
____	0.8	____	5.8
____	0.99	____	0.08

Trick # 7 TAIL WHEELIE

____	0.0001	____	0.000001
____	0.001	____	0.01
____	101.1	____	10.11
____	1.1	____	0.00011

Name

A HUGE OBSTACLE COURSE

A runner in the steeplechase race has to run 3,000 meters and jump over 28 hurdles and 7 water jumps. See if you can get past all the obstacles on this course!

At each jump, compare the decimals. Insert the correct symbol (>, <, or =) to show how the numbers compare.

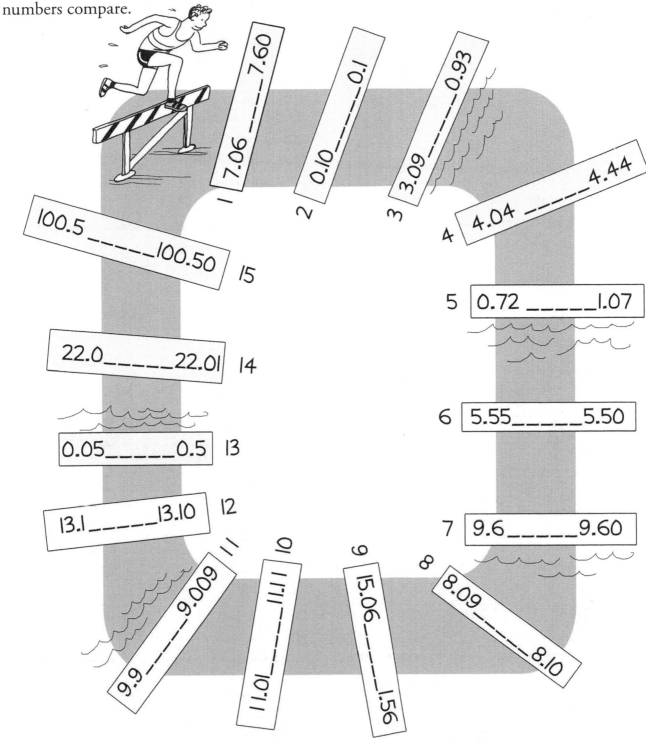

1 7.06 _____ 7.60

2 0.10 _____ 0.1

3 3.09 _____ 0.93

4 4.04 _____ 4.44

5 0.72 _____ 1.07

6 5.55 _____ 5.50

7 9.6 _____ 9.60

8 8.09 _____ 8.10

9 15.06 _____ 1.56

10 11.11 _____ 11.01

11 9.9 _____ 9.009

12 13.1 _____ 13.10

13 0.05 _____ 0.5

14 22.0 _____ 22.01

15 100.5 _____ 100.50

Name

Common Core Reinforcement Activities — 4th Grade Math

WHO WEARS THE MEDALS?

In the Olympics, the individual all-around championship is the highest achievement a gymnast can reach. Most gymnasts dream of winning this gold medal. Gymnasts must compete in four events. Their scores from all four events are totaled to see who has the highest score.

Add up the scores for all these gymnasts. Then rank them in order from first to last.

Gymnast	Balance Beam	Floor Exercise	Uneven Bars	Horse Vault	Total Score	Place
Karin	9.932	9.912	9.955	9.680		
Sofia	9.817	9.950	9.609	9.896		
Elena	8.954	9.987	9.640	9.320		
Kim	8.999	9.690	9.800	9.975		
Kerri	9.981	9.208	9.997	9.700		
Tatiana	9.975	10.00	9.980	9.973		
Nina	9.290	9.964	9.699	9.609		
Larissa	9.956	9.866	9.057	9.666		
Svetlana	9.979	9.979	9.780	10.00		
Olga	8.974	9.401	8.899	9.789		
Kathy	10.00	9.777	9.780	9.925		
Tamara	9.966	10.00	9.224	9.099		

Who won the Gold? _____

Silver? _____ Bronze? _____

Name _____

"FIGURING" OUT DECIMALS

Tamara is tracing a figure eight to practice precise skating. For many years, figures were part of the score in figure skating competitions. Figures were eliminated from competitions after 1990.

Practice your decimal skills by finding the decimal in Tamara's figure eight that solves each problem.

_____ 1. one-tenth more than 7 RED

_____ 2. five-hundredths more than 6.3 BLUE

_____ 3. the difference between 10.8 and 10.2 PINK

_____ 4. one hundred plus twelve-hundredths BLACK

_____ 5. 3 tenths more than 6 hundredths YELLOW

_____ 6. 0.05 plus 0.04 PURPLE

_____ 7. 9 tenths less than ten TAN

_____ 8. two-tenths more than 14 ORANGE

_____ 9. 5 hundredths more than 2 BROWN

_____ 10. one-tenth less than one TAN

_____ 11. two-tenths plus four-hundredths SILVER

_____ 12. 9 tenths plus 9 hundredths GREEN

_____ 13. ten plus twelve-hundredths RED

_____ 14. eight-hundredths more than eight BLUE

_____ 15. one-tenth less than ten GREEN

_____ 16. two-tenths less than nine PINK

_____ 17. ten less than 12.4 PURPLE

_____ 18. 0.004 more than 0.005 RED

_____ 19. ten less than 10.22 ORANGE

_____ 20. 0.6 more than three YELLOW

_____ 21. two-tenths more than 0.3 BLUE

_____ 22. 5 tenths less than fifty-one GREEN

_____ 23. five-tenths less than 21 SILVER

_____ 24. one hundred plus two-tenths PURPLE

Name _____

A GREAT MATCH!

Tennis started in the thirteenth century in France. Players stretched a cord of rope across a room and hit a cloth bag full of hair back and forth over the rope! Now tennis is an Olympic sport with four events that include singles and doubles matches for men and women. Tennis is a very active sport. Players run back and forth across the court through the whole match.

— Olympic Fact —

Tennis balls are made from rubber molded into 2 cups that are cemented together and covered with wool.

A new tennis ball can bounce about 55 feet.

Draw a path for each of these players to run around on her side of the court.
Draw a line from the player through the decimal numerals in order from smallest to largest.

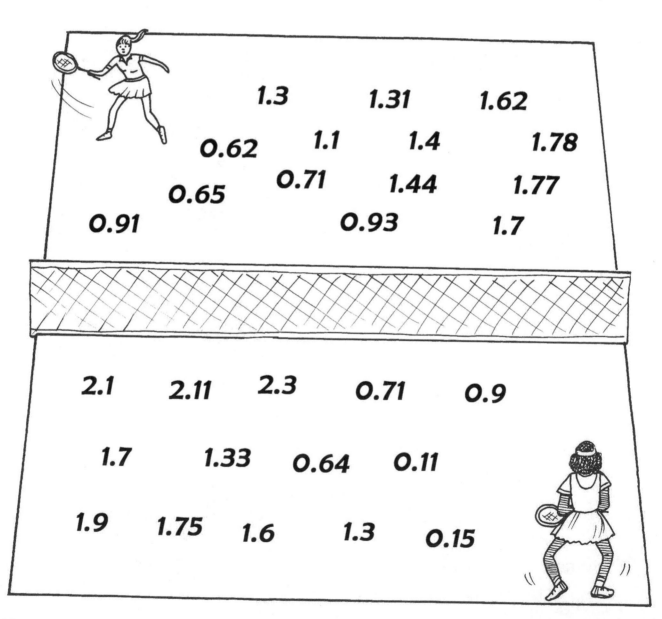

MEASUREMENT
AND
DATA

Grade 4

MORE OR LESS?

Ooops! The weightlifters have a problem at practice today. The weights on both ends of the bars are not equal for every athlete!

Look at the measurement amounts below. They have the same problem.
Compare the measures. Write > (greater than), < (less than), or = in each circle.

1. 6 pt ◯ 3 qt

2. 16 oz ◯ 1 lb

3. 9 qt ◯ 16 pt

4. 5 pt ◯ 10 c

5. 3 ft ◯ 36 in

6. 3 lb ◯ 59 oz

7. 2 c ◯ 1 pt

8. 2 lb ◯ 22 oz

9. 7 yd ◯ 21 ft

10. 2,000 lb ◯ 1 T

11. 12 ft ◯ 3 yd

12. 6 gal ◯ 18 qt

13. 38 in ◯ 1 yd

14. 4 yd ◯ 100 in

15. 2 qt ◯ 8 gal

16. 11 in ◯ 1 ft

17. 4 t ◯ 6 tsp

18. 100 sec ◯ 2 min

19. 7 hr ◯ 420 min

20. 10 gal ◯ 40 qt

Name

86

MEASUREMENT SENSE

It's time for Matt to get a new soccer uniform. Today he got measured to find out exactly what size he needs. His friend Sam took the measurement.

Answer these questions about his measurements and other soccer measurements.

1. Sam says the circumference of Matt's head is 2 feet, 11 inches. Is this a reasonable measurement? _____

2. Matt measured from Matt's shoulder to the tip of his finger. The distance is 2 feet, 1 inch. Matt says this was 25 inches. Is he right? _____

3. Matt's soccer socks are 21 inches from top to toe. Matt thinks this is almost 2 feet long. Is he right? _____

4. Matt and Sam's middle school soccer field is 110 meters long. Sam says this is 1,100 centimeters long. Is he right? _____

5. Yesterday's soccer game began at 1:15 p.m. It ended at 2:40 p.m. Matt thinks this amount of time is 125 minutes. Is he right? _____

6. The diameter of Matt's soccer ball is 22 centimeters. Sam says this is 220 meters. Is he right? _____

7. Each of Sam's new soccer shoes weighs 10.1 ounces. He is sure that he is carrying around about five pounds. Is this reasonable? _____

8. At the end of the game, each of the 10 players drinks 1500 milliliters of water. Sam calculated that this equals 15 liters of water. Is he right? _____

9. Sam's soccer bag, full of all his stuff, weighs 1,900 grams. Matt says this is almost 2 kilograms. Is he right? _____

10. The soccer team travels 68 kilometers to a game. Sam says this is 680 meters. Matt says this is 6,800 centimeters. Who's right? _____

Name _____

Common Core Reinforcement Activities — 4th Grade Math

PASSING THE TEST

In most schools, athletes must keep good grades in order to play a school sport. How is Tom doing on his measurement test? He needs to have 9 correct in order to pass the test.

Circle the numbers of the correct answers. Cross out the wrong answers and replace them with the correct answers.

Measurement Test

Student Name: **Tom**   Date: **January 6**

1. Liquids are measured in __*meters*__ .
2. Would 5 milliliters of water fill a cup? yes (no)
3. Circle the greater amount: (10 kilograms) 100 grams
4. Could someone's hand be 1 decimeter long? (yes) no
5. Circle the larger amount: 2 kilometers (200 meters)
6. 1 meter = __*100*__ centimeters.
7. 1 kilometer = __*1,000*__ meters.
8. __*100*__ milliliters = 1 liter.
9. 100 meters = __*1*__ decimeter(s).
10. 5 grams = __*5,000*__ milligrams.
11. 20 meters = __*2*__ centimeters.
12. __*300*__ centimeters = 3 meters.
13. 1 metric ton = __*1,000*__ kilograms.
14. 1 gram = __*100*__ milligrams.
15. 10 kilometers = __*500*__ meters.
16. 10,000 milligrams = __*10*__ grams.

I'm sure I'll pass the test.

Will Tom pass? _____

Name

OUTLANDISH MEASUREMENTS

Search the tennis court to solve the tennis problems.

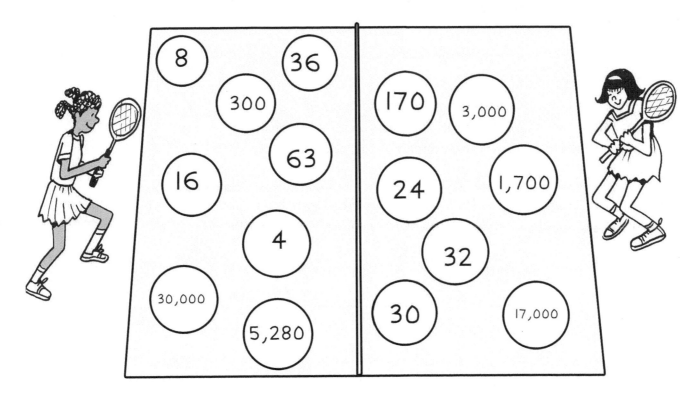

Fill in each blank with the correct number from one of the balls.

1. length of a 2-ft racquet = _____ in

2. 1-mi distance run = _____ ft

3. energy drink of 2 qt = _____ c

4. 2-lb bottle of sunscreen = _____ oz

5. weight of 3-kg sports bag = _____ dg

6. height of 3-ft tennis net = _____ in

7. weight of 3-L jug of juice = _____ kL

8. length of
30-km bus trip = _____ m

9. tennis court
width of 17 m = _____ cm

10. 2-gal jug of water = _____ pt

11. 17 g weight of
3 tennis balls = _____ mg

12. height of
5 ft, 3 in player = _____ in

Name _____

Common Core Reinforcement Activities — 4th Grade Math

JUST IN CASE

Just in case anyone has wondered about Mochaville Middle School's athletic abilities, the proof of their excellence can be found in the school trophy case. Just step into the lobby of the gym and take a look.

Look closely at these trophies! Each one holds a measurement. Several pairs of trophies have measurements that stand for the same amount. Choose 10 different colors of markers or crayons. Color the pairs of matching measurements with the same color.

Name

MEASUREMENTS ON PARADE

The Booster Club members are building floats and getting ready for a big sports parade. There's lots of measuring needed! Solve the measurement problems. Circle one answer.

1. Each float uses about 2.5 gal of paint. There are 12 floats. How many quarts will be used?

   a. 120   b. 125   c. 30

2. The tuba in the band is 20 cm less than one m tall. This is

   a. 8 cm   b. 80 cm   c. 8,000 cm

3. The Booster Club sells popcorn at the parade. Each box of popcorn weighs 80 g. 60 boxes of popcorn are sold. Together, they weigh

   a. 4.8 kg   b. 48 kg   c. 480 kg

4. It takes the band $5\frac{1}{4}$ minutes to play the opening song. They play 3 more songs of 5 minutes each during the parade. All together, the band plays

   a. 35 sec

   b. 1,350 sec

   c. 1,215 sec

5. The first five floats are each about $8\frac{1}{2}$ ft long. A distance of $4\frac{1}{2}$ ft separates them. What is the distance from the front of the first float to the end of the fifth float?

   a. 50 ft   b. 60 ft   c. neither of these

6. It takes about 150 hr to prepare for the parade. The parade lasts 140 min. What is the difference between these times?

   a. 10 min   b. 8,860 min   c. neither of these

7. Last year, float builders bought 35 L of glue for gluing decorations onto the floats. This year they bought three times that much. How much did they buy this year?

   a. 1.5 kL   b. 105 L   c. 1,050 mL

8. This year's parade route is $\frac{3}{4}$ mi long. Last year's route was 4,250 ft long. Which route is the longest?

   a. this year's

   b. last year's

   c. They are the same length

Name _____

CHILL OUT

Athletes drink lots of refreshing drinks, use plenty of towels, and get many uniforms dirty. You won't need to know an exact answer for these problems about their drinks, towels, and uniforms. Sometimes a close answer is just fine!

Practice your estimation skills by circling the closest answer.

1. Each kid on the track team drinks $2\frac{1}{2}$ gallons of water at each meet. There are 12 on the team. How much water do they drink each meet?

   10 gal   50 gal   30 gal   24 gal

2. There are 8 tug-of-war teams with 11 players each. Every player uses 2 towels. It takes $\frac{1}{10}$ c of soap powder to wash each towel. About how many cups of soap are needed to wash these towels?

   9   17   21   15

3. Each drinking cup at the snack shack gets filled with about $\frac{1}{4}$ cup of ice. On Sunday, 20 cups of ice were used. How many drinking cups were used?

   4   80   120   40

4. After the game, the football team uses a lot of deodorant. Each player uses 2.4 g under each arm. There are 26 players. About how much deodorant is used?

   130 g   35 g   7500 g   300 g

5. A 5-gallon jug of SLAM Sports Drink serves about 30 thirsty kids. If 92 kids show up at Field Day, about how many jugs will be needed?

   30   50   3   300

6. Three kids on the relay team made T-shirts to replace the worn-out shirts for their team. They bought the shirts for $3 and sold them for $5.95. If they bought 30 shirts and sold them all, about how much money did they make?

   $900 $190 $90 $180

7. At the end of the season, the baseball coach found 3 lockers full of smelly socks. Each locker held 38 pairs of socks. He decided to burn the socks. He threw each pair into the fire one at a time. Each one took about $\frac{3}{4}$ min to burn. About how long did it take all the socks to burn?

   120 min $1\frac{1}{2}$ hr $2\frac{1}{2}$ hr   1 hr

8. If ten runners each wear out four pairs of $92.75 shoes a year, about how much will they spend on shoes all together?

   $372 $3,700 $930 $9,275

9. Ten racers each ran 1,500 kilometers. How far was their total distance?

   15,000 m   15,000,000 m
   15,000 cm   1,500,000 m

Name

AMAZING FEET

Athletes do amazing things with their feet, and they wear all kinds of interesting footwear while they do these feats! Solve the feet problems by circling **yes** or **no** for each question.

1. An ice skater skated 30 laps around the outside of a rink that measured 100 by 200 ft. Would she have skated about 90,000 ft?

YES   NO

2. A biker drank 12.65 L water during one race. Is that more than 12,600 mL of water?

YES   NO

3. This ski boot has traveled 12,000 km up and down ski hills. Is that distance greater than 5,000,000 m?

YES   NO

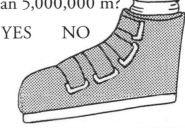

4. The basketball player who wore this shoe weighed 223 lb Is that 112 oz less than a player who weighed 225 lb?

YES   NO

5. This sock has held five toes that average a length of 6.8 cm. Is the total length of the toes greater than 35 cm?

YES   NO

6. A hiker covered 3,000 mi of trails in this boot. Is this distance greater than 15 million ft?

YES   NO

7. This shoe was worn with seven different dancing dresses. Each one of them cost $85.25. Could it be said that the dancer spent about $450 on these dresses?

YES   NO

8. If this soccer shoe weighed 4.3 oz, would 6 pairs of these same shoes weigh over 8 lb?

YES   NO

9. This flipper has been under water for a total of 960 hrs. All together, does this time total more than a month?

YES   NO

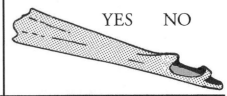

10. If all the costs of skating (and the equipment) average $1.10 per hr of skating, and the skater has $300, can the skater enjoy 250 hrs of skating?   YES   NO

11. Each time the athlete takes a step on the snowshoe, he lifts 12 g of powdery snow. With 100 steps, will he lift more than 1 kg of powder?

YES   NO

Name

Common Core Reinforcement Activities — 4th Grade Math

DIAMONDS, RINGS, AND COURTS

Athletes do plenty of running around, swimming along, shooting across, or working on big surfaces. How far is it around the field, arena, or location of their sport? What area is covered by the places they compete?

Choose the right formula from the center to find the perimeter and area of the figures.

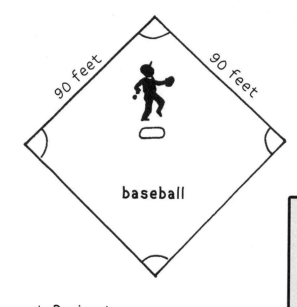

90 feet   90 feet

baseball

1. Perimeter = _____

   Area = _____

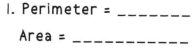

16 feet

boxing

16 feet

2. Perimeter = _____

   Area = _____

Formulas for Perimeter

polygon   P = sum of sides
circle   P = πd

Formulas for Area

square   A = s²
rectangle A = lw
circle   A = πr²
triangle   A = ½ bh
trapezoid A = $\frac{h(b_1 + b_2)}{2}$

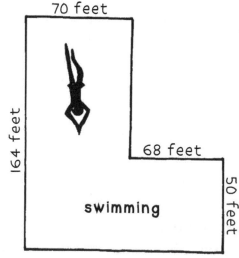

70 feet

164 feet

68 feet

50 feet

swimming

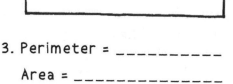

3. Perimeter = _____

   Area = _____

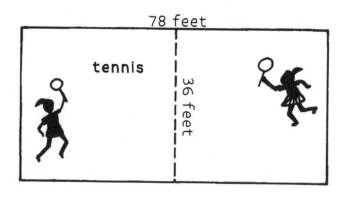

78 feet

tennis

36 feet

4. Perimeter = _____

   Area = _____

Use with page 95.

Name

Choose the right formula from the center to find the perimeter and area of the figures.

75 feet

15 feet

archery

5. Perimeter = ------------

Area = -----------------

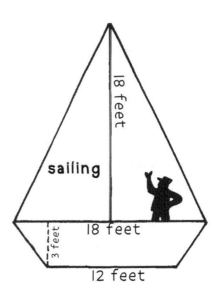

sailing

18 feet

3 feet   18 feet

12 feet

6. Area =_____

Formulas for Perimeter

| polygon | $P = $ sum of sides |
| circle | $P = \pi d$ |

Formulas for Area

square	$A = s^2$
rectangle	$A = lw$
circle	$A = \pi r^2$
triangle	$A = \frac{1}{2} bh$
trapezoid	$A = \dfrac{h(b_1 + b_2)}{2}$

600 feet

wrestling

12 feet

track

200 feet

7. Perimeter = _____

Area = _____

8. Perimeter = _____

Area = _____

Use with page 94.

Name

Copyright © 2014 World Book, Inc./
Incentive Publications, Chicago, IL

Common Core Reinforcement Activities — 4th Grade Math

DUFFEL BAG JUMBLE

Jadyn just came home from tennis practice and dumped the contents of his duffel bag on the floor. Everything in the bag is a geometric plane figure or a space figure. Use the right formula to find the perimeter or area of some of these figures or some of their sides.

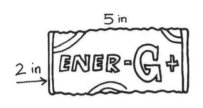

1. Area of top of energy bar = _____

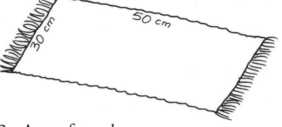

Formulas

P of polygon = sum of all sides
P of circle = πd
A of circle = $πr_2$
A of rectangle = lw
A of square = s_2

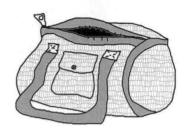

2. Area of towel = _____
   Perimeter = _____

4. Perimeter of top of box = _____

3. Area of top page of magazine = _____

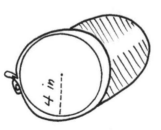

6. Area of top of tennis ball can = _____

5. Perimeter of inside of cap circle = _____

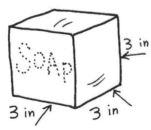

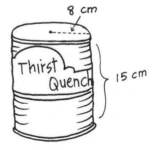

8. Area of top of Thirst Quench can = _____

7. Area of one face of soap cube = _____

Name _____

RECORD-SETTING SWALLOWING

People swallow large amounts of food items extremely fast to set food-eating records. They gobble up things such as pancakes, spaghetti, hot dogs, whole lemons, raw eggs, pickled onions, pizza, baked beans, cow brains, and pigs' feet!

Review the table with information about the number of raw onions competitors ate in a 2-minute competition. Represent this data on the line plot.

Onions Eaten at Competition

Name	# of Onions	Name	# of Onions	Name	# of Onions
Amee	5	Lou	3	Denise	1
Lasa	4	Maya	2	Harry	2
Geogio	6	Tasha	2	Ramon	2
Lane	2	DeShaun	5	Sue	4
Tomas	1	Evan	1	Jenna	5.5
Marita	6	Scott	5	Kris	3
Anya	6	Ryan	3.5	Lucy	6
Blake	4	Lee	3	Todd	5
Chou	5	Vonna	4	Rob	5

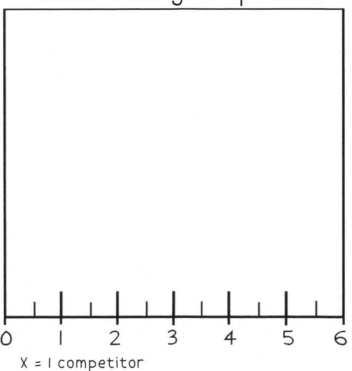

Onion-Eating Competition

0   1   2   3   4   5   6

X = 1 competitor

Name _____

WONDERFUL WALLS

It may sound unbelievable, but someone has built a wall out of bubbles! Fan-Yang of Canada built the record-setting bubble wall in 1997. It was 156 feet long and it stayed up for about 5–10 seconds.

The line plot shows the frequency of times other bubble walls lasted. Each x represents one bubble wall. The numbers on the line stand for the number of seconds walls lasted. Use the plot to answer the questions.

1. How many walls lasted 5 seconds? _____

2. How many walls lasted fewer than 4 seconds? _____

3. What time lengths show the same number of walls? _____

4. How many walls are represented here? _____

5. What was the total number of walls lasting 4 through 7 seconds? _____

6. Do you see any patterns in the data?

_____

_____

_____

_____

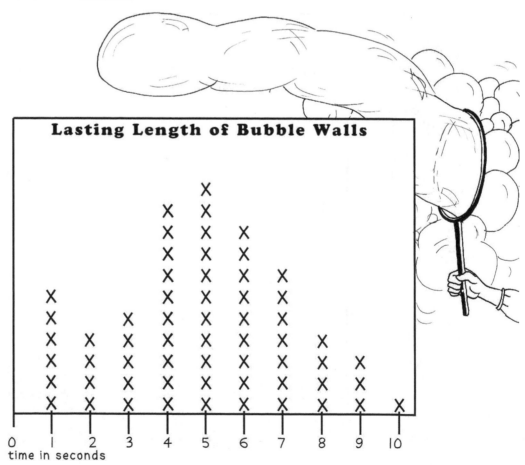

Lasting Length of Bubble Walls

time in seconds

Name _____

CRAZY COMPETITIONS

People do lots of weird tricks in competition! The clock is ticking while they kill mosquitoes, juggle flaming torches, spit watermelon seeds, toss and spin pizza dough, and other wacky feats!

A family of pizza-dough tossers has many competitors. Cousins, mothers, grandparents, kids, aunts and uncles, and siblings all know the skill. The line plot shows data for the number of minutes each of these relatives usually keeps the dough in the air.

1. How many relatives keep dough in the air for 8 or 10 minutes? _____

2. What is the difference between the time with the most competitors and the time with the least? _____

3. How many keep the dough in the air more than 6 minutes? _____

4. How many keep the dough in the air less than 5 minutes? _____

5. How many relatives are included in the data? _____

6. How many relatives keep dough in the air for 2 or 9 minutes? _____

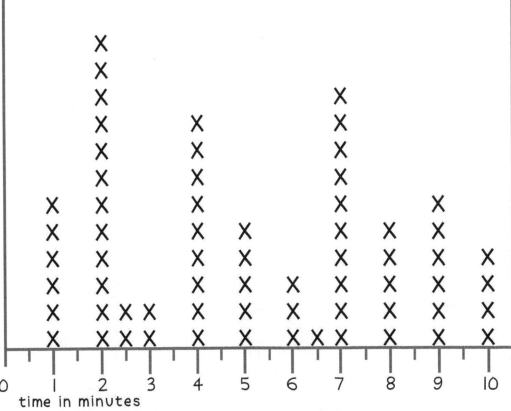

time in minutes

Name _____

Common Core Reinforcement Activities — 4th Grade Math

DEEP-SEA DATA

Scuba divers descend to different depths. A line plot can be used to keep data on several divers. This line plot shows depth in feet to which a group of divers descended during one day's dive. Each X represents one diver. Use the data shown on the line plot to answer the questions.

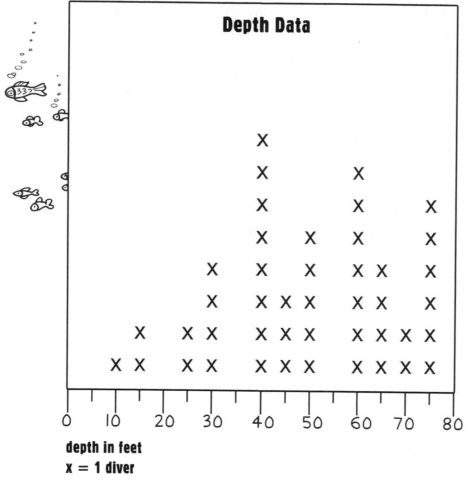

Depth Data

depth in feet

x = 1 diver

1. How many divers are shown in this data? _____

2. What is the difference between the shallowest and deepest dive in the data? _____

3. How many divers went deeper than 50 ft? _____

4. How many divers went deeper than 75 ft? _____

5. Which span of distance had the most divers: > 30 < 65   or   > 50 < 75? _____

Use with page 101.

Name

Many people dive for the joy of seeing the underwater creatures. The list gives information about lengths of underwater creatures this diver saw. Create a line plot to show this data.

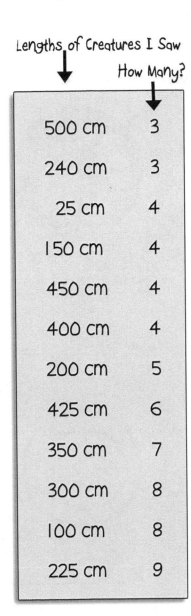

Lengths of Creatures I Saw	How Many?
500 cm	3
240 cm	3
25 cm	4
150 cm	4
450 cm	4
400 cm	4
200 cm	5
425 cm	6
350 cm	7
300 cm	8
100 cm	8
225 cm	9

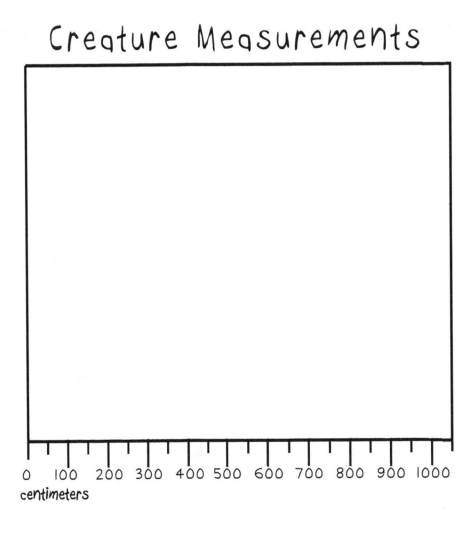

Creature Measurements

0   100   200   300   400   500   600   700   800   900   1000

centimeters

Use with page 100.

Name _____

WATCHING THE TIME

Time plays a part in most sports. Coaches, fans, players, and referees are always watching the clock!

The hands on each of these clocks form an angle. Measure the angle that is shown by the arrow. Write the measurement on the line. Round it to the nearest 5 degrees.

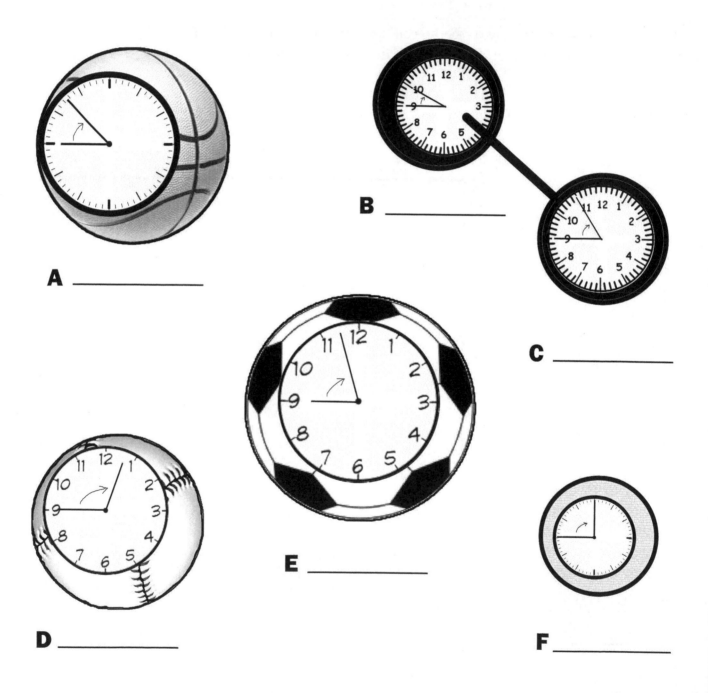

A _____

B _____

C _____

D _____

E _____

F _____

Use with page 103.

Name

WATCHING THE TIME, continued

Keep watching the clocks!

Measure the angle that is shown by the arrow on each clock. Write the measurement on the line. Round it to the nearest 5 degrees.

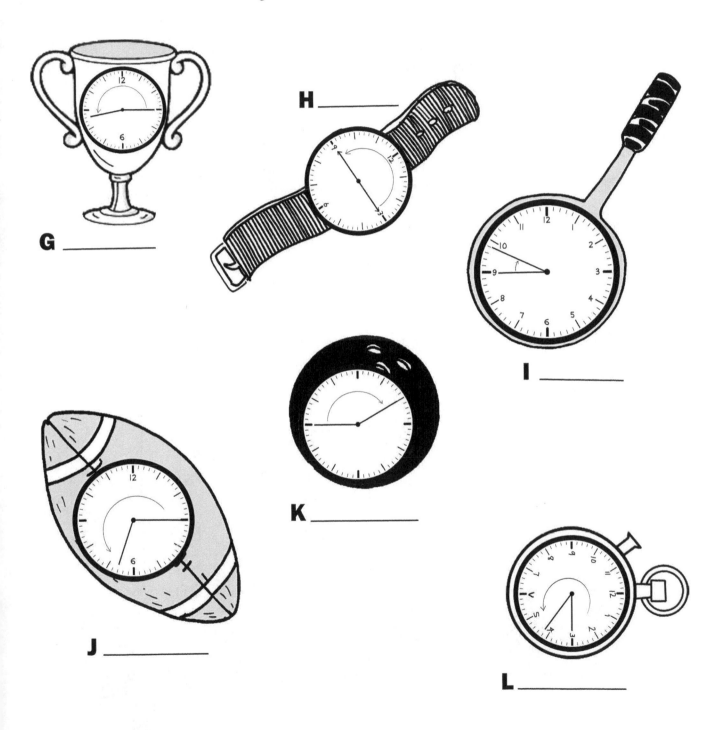

G _____

H _____

I _____

J _____

K _____

L _____

Use with page 102.

Name _____

ANGLES AT THE POOL

For divers, good form is very important. They must hold their bodies at exactly the right angles! Deva keeps a chart of the body positions for her different dives.

Look at the angles shown on the chart. Then take the plunge and circle the best estimate for the measurement of each angle.

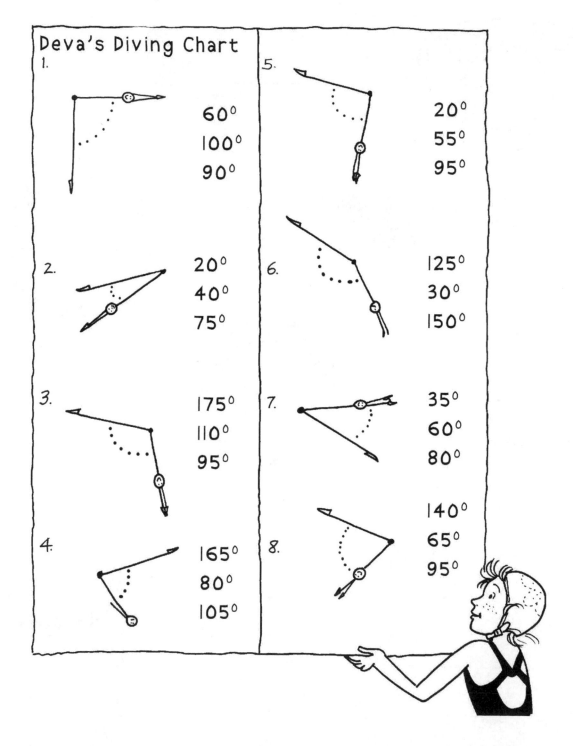

Deva's Diving Chart

1. 60°   100°   90°

2. 20°   40°   75°

3. 175°   110°   95°

4. 165°   80°   105°

5. 20°   55°   95°

6. 125°   30°   150°

7. 35°   60°   80°

8. 140°   65°   95°

Name

ANGLES AT THE GYM

Angles show up a lot at the gym, too. Gymnasts must pay attention to good form. Notice the sharp angles that gymnasts hold as they perform their routines.

Use a protractor to measure each angle shown on the chart. Write the measurement to the nearest whole degree.

1. _____ °

2. _____ °
   (left)

   _____ °
   (right)

3. _____ °

4. _____ °
   (left)

   _____ °
   (right)

5. _____ °
   (left)

   _____ °
   (right)

6. _____ °

7. _____ °

8. _____ °
   (above leg)

   _____ °
   (below leg)

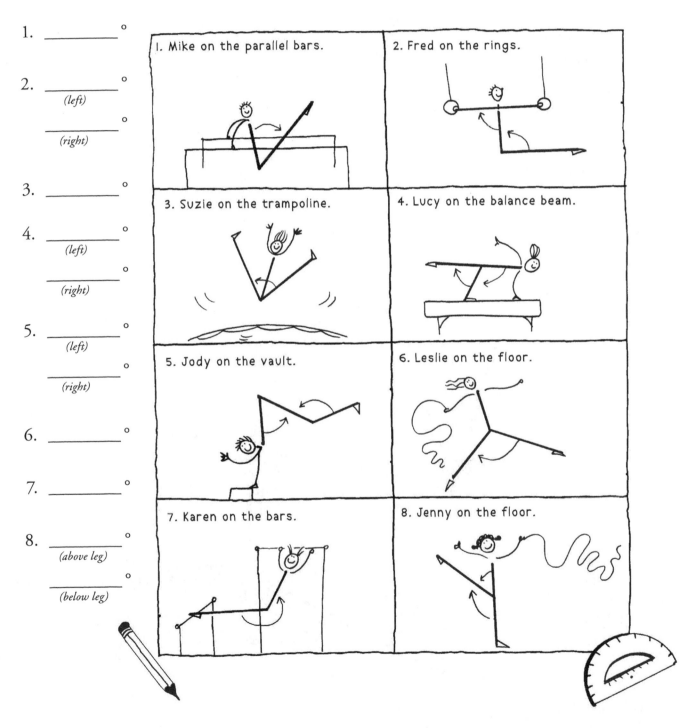

1. Mike on the parallel bars.

2. Fred on the rings.

3. Suzie on the trampoline.

4. Lucy on the balance beam.

5. Jody on the vault.

6. Leslie on the floor.

7. Karen on the bars.

8. Jenny on the floor.

Name _____

Common Core Reinforcement Activities — 4th Grade Math

WHAT'S THE ANGLE?

Some of the cross-country ski team members did a poor job of putting away their skis! The skis are criss-crossing each other at many different angles.

Measure each numbered angle. Round the measurement to the nearest whole degree. Write it in the angle. Then solve problems 1–4.

1. What is the sum of angles 1 and 2? _____ °

2. What is the sum of angles 3 and 4? _____ °

3. What is the sum of angles 7 and 8? _____ °

4. What is the difference between angles 5 and 6? _____ °

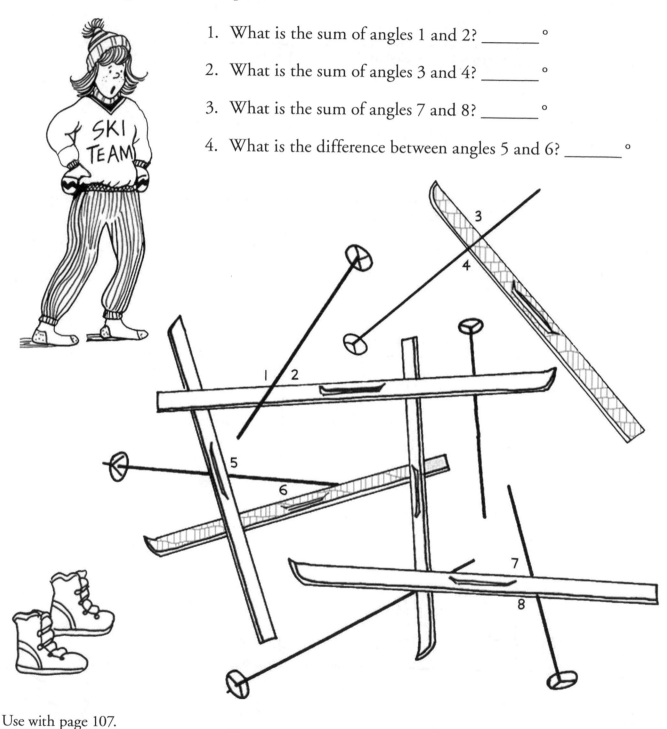

Use with page 107.

Name

Measure each numbered angle. Round to the nearest whole degree. Write the measurement in the angle. Then solve problems 5–8.

5. What is the sum of angles 9 and 10? _____°

6. What is the difference between angle 11 and angle 12? _____°

7. What is the sum of angles 13, 14, and 15? _____°

8. What is the sum of angles 16, 17, 18, and 19? _____°

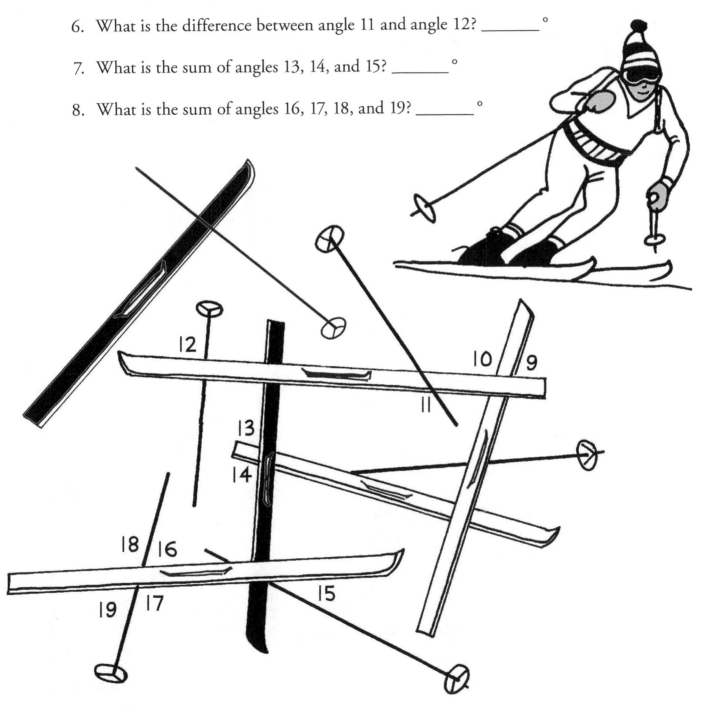

Use with page 106.

Name _____

Common Core Reinforcement Activities — 4th Grade Math

ANGLES IN EQUIPMENT

Angles show up in many pieces of sports equipment. Notice the angles in each of these items!

Measure each angle shown by the dotted line. Round the measurement to the nearest 5°. Write the angle measurement on the line by the item number.

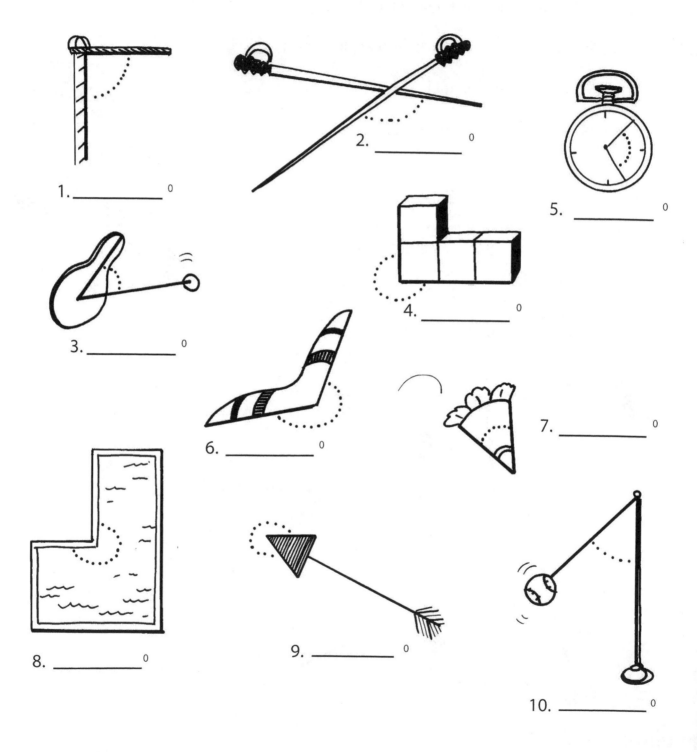

1. _____ 0

2. _____ 0

3. _____ 0

4. _____ 0

5. _____ 0

6. _____ 0

7. _____ 0

8. _____ 0

9. _____ 0

10. _____ 0

Name

GET SHARP WITH ANGLES

The design on the karate mat is formed by many angles. Polish up your computation skills to get sharp with angles!

Add or subtract to find measurements in the problems below. Do not use a protractor! (Remember that a straight line is a 180° angle.)

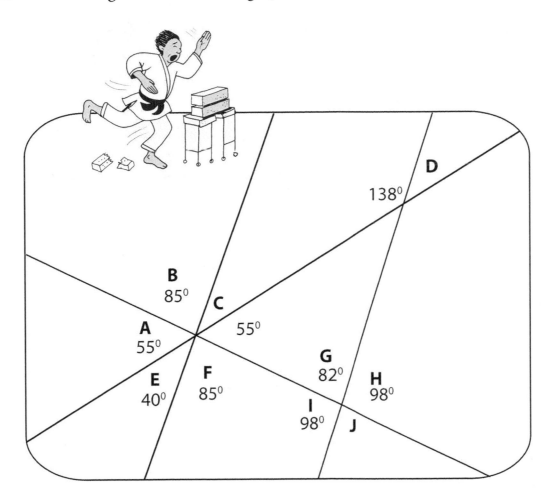

1. $\angle A + \angle B =$ _____ °

2. $\angle C =$ _____ °

3. $\angle H - \angle G =$ _____ °

4. $\angle F + \angle B =$ _____ °

5. $\angle A + \angle E + \angle F =$ _____ °

6. $\angle I + \angle G =$ _____ °

7. $\angle D =$ _____ °

8. $\angle G + \angle H + \angle I + \angle J =$ _____ °

Use with page 110.

Name

Common Core Reinforcement Activities — 4th Grade Math

The design on the weightlifter's mat is formed by many angles. Polish up your computation skills to get sharp with angles!

Add or subtract to find measurements in the problems below. Do not use a protractor! (Remember that a straight line is a 180° angle.)

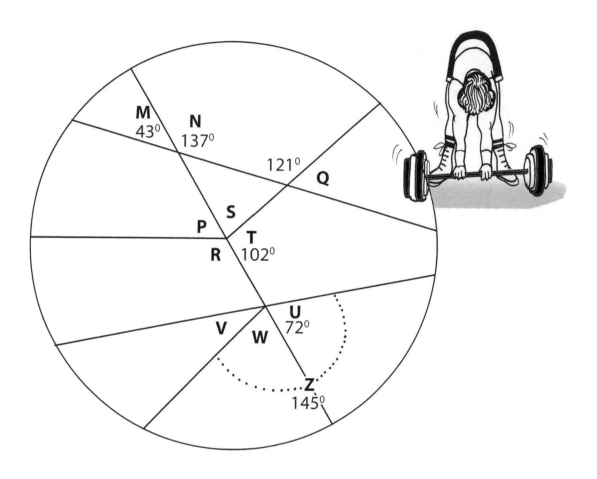

9. $\angle M + \angle N =$ _____ °

10. $\angle Q =$ _____ °

11. $\angle R + \angle P =$ _____ °

12. $\angle S =$ _____ °

13. $\angle P + \angle R + \angle S + \angle T =$ _____ °

14. $\angle S + \angle T =$ _____ °

15. $\angle Z - \angle U =$ _____ °

16. $\angle V + \angle W + \angle U =$ _____ °

Use with page 109.

Name

GEOMETRY

Grade 4

SIGNS FROM THE CROWD

The rowdy crowd is getting ready for the opening football game of the season between the Ashland Grizzlies and the Crescent City Cougars.

Draw a line from each label to match the correct sign.

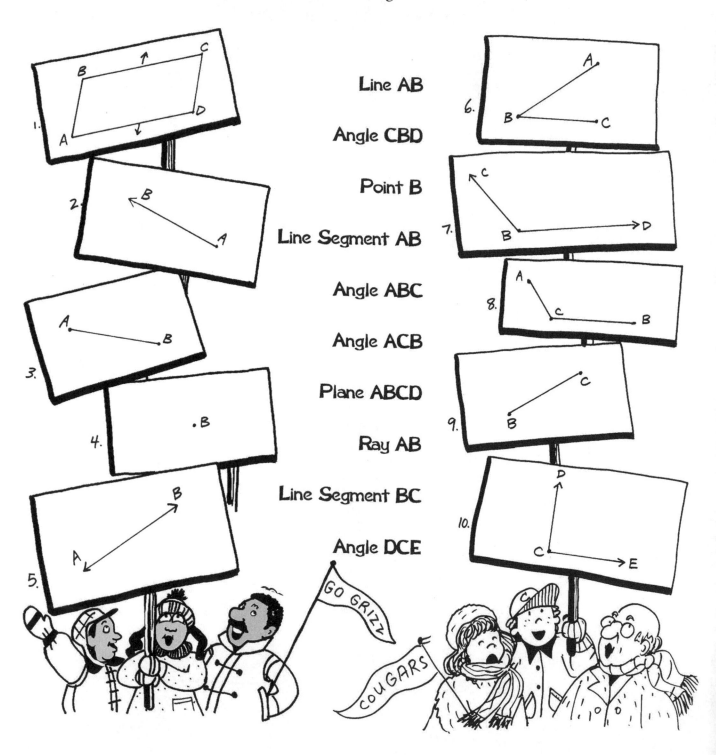

Line AB

Angle CBD

Point B

Line Segment AB

Angle ABC

Angle ACB

Plane ABCD

Ray AB

Line Segment BC

Angle DCE

Name

BANNER GEOMETRY

Geometry shows up in all kinds of places, even the new Grizzly team banner offers a good place for a geometry review! Color the banner with the Grizzly colors of red, white, and light blue. (You decide where the colors look best.) Then answer the geometry questions.

1. How many line segments can you find? _____ List the line segments here.

   _____

   _____

   _____

   _____

   _____

2. How many angles can you find? _____ List them here.

   _____

   _____

   _____

   _____

3. Write your initials in the vertex of angle RNO.

Name _____

Common Core Reinforcement Activities — 4th Grade Math

GEOMETRY AT THE BALL PARK

Take your markers to the ballpark for the first home game and search the scene for geometric places and spaces.

Color or trace at least three of each figure.
Use the color chart to find the right color for each one.

FIGURE	COLOR
point	blue
plane	green
line segment	red
angle	yellow

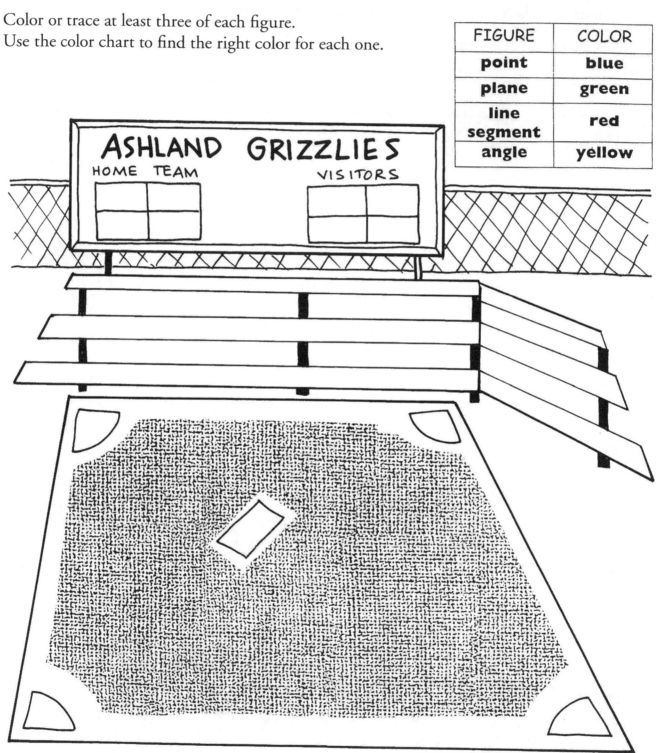

LOCKER ROOM MYSTERY

The lockers in the Ashland Middle School locker room have unusual names on them!
Can you figure out which locker belongs to which athlete?

Write the letter of the locker that matches each clue.

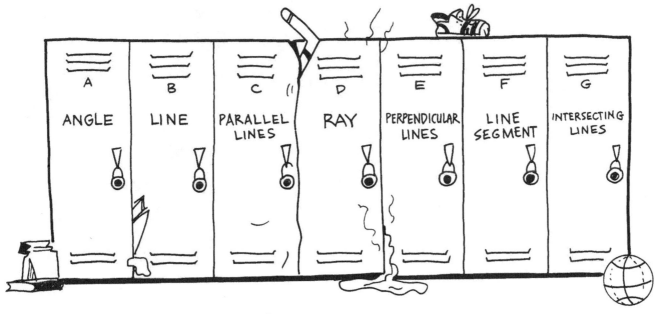

Clues

_____ 1. Ashley's Locker   I'm part of a line that has only one endpoint.

_____ 2. Sara's Locker   We are lines in the same plane, but we never met.

_____ 3. Gina's Locker   I am made of two rays that have the same end point.

_____ 4. Kate's Locker   I am part of a line that has two endpoints.

_____ 5. Gayle's Locker   I extend in opposite directions without end.

_____ 6. Kayla's Locker   When we meet another line, it is always at a right angle.

_____ 7. Megan's Locker   The two of us meet and cross each other.

8. Draw a pair of perpendicular lines.	9. Draw a pair of intersecting lines.	10. Draw a pair of parallel lines.

Name _____

Common Core Reinforcement Activities — 4th Grade Math

NEW ANGLES ON CHEERS

The cheerleaders are practicing for the first pep rally.
They're practicing some new tricks and routines.

1. Name all the acute angles.

    _____

    _____

2. Name all the right angles.

    _____

    _____

3. Name all the obtuse angles.

    _____

    _____

    _____

Name

116

GYM FLOOR GEOMETRY

The Booster Club spent a year collecting money for a new gym floor. What a job! Student groups were asked to submit designs for the floor. Here is the prizewinning design. It's full of triangles. Can you find them all?

Follow the chart to color the floor design.

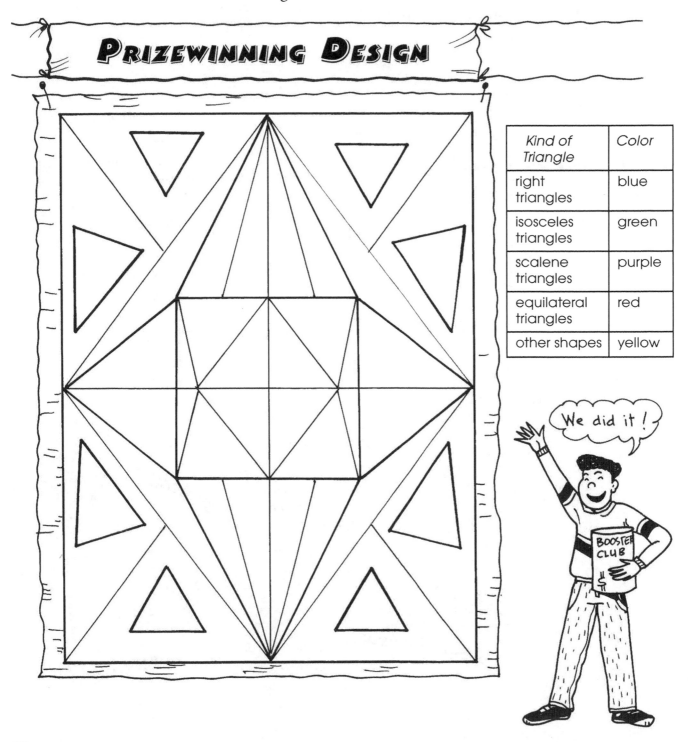

Kind of Triangle	Color
right triangles	blue
isosceles triangles	green
scalene triangles	purple
equilateral triangles	red
other shapes	yellow

Name _____

Common Core Reinforcement Activities — 4th Grade Math

A PLANE MESS

Coach Jackson teaches math when he is not coaching volleyball. He had some great posters ready for his geometry lesson today, but, as usual, he forgot to close the window. A huge wind blew his stuff all over the floor.

Get the definition posters back together with the math terms in time for class. Draw a line from each math term to its matching poster.

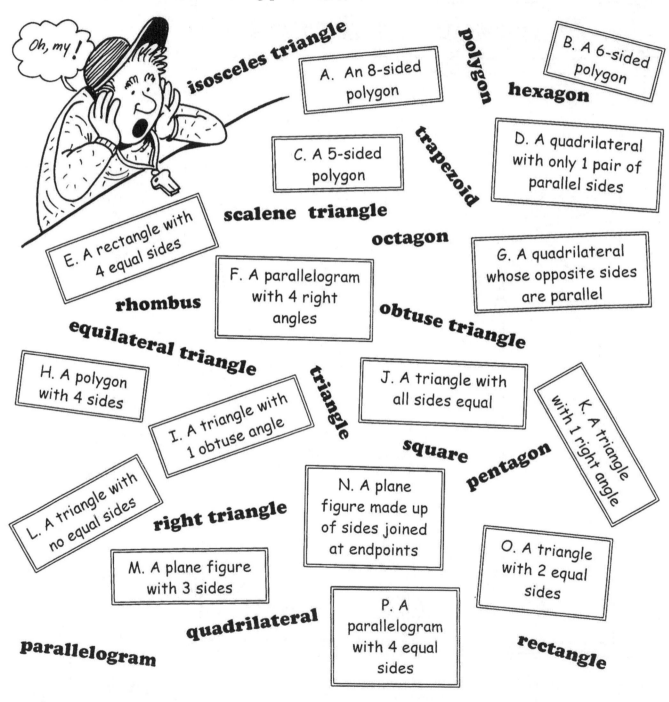

Name

SHARP EYE FOR SHAPES

There is a piece of hidden sports equipment in this picture. Do you know what it is?

To find out, follow the color chart to color each figure. Because some shapes fit more than one definition, color each shape in the order indicated on the chart.

Polygon	Color
Octagons	Blue
Pentagons	Black
Hexagons	Pink
Squares	Green
Rectangles	Purple
Triangles	Aqua
Rhombuses	Brown
Trapezoids	Red
Parallelograms	Yellow
Quadrilaterals	Orange

1. What is it? _____

2. In which sport is this object used? _____

Name _____

Common Core Reinforcement Activities — 4th Grade Math

GOING IN CIRCLES

The wrestling team is warming up for their big match against their rivals, the Crescent City Cougars. The athletes will show off their wrestling skills on a circular mat with a diameter of 11 meters.

Use the circle diagram of the mat to show off your geometry skills and knowledge about the parts of a circle.

1. The team captain, Will, will stand at the center. What point is this? _____

2. Jason and Dan warm up by jogging back and forth on the diameters. Name the diameters.

   _____

3. Geoff will warm up by jogging back and forth on each radius. Name the radii.

   _____

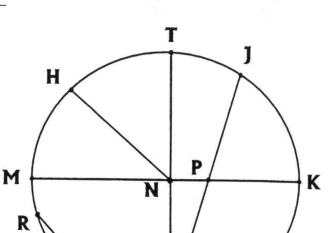

4. Chris will jump rope along 2 chords. Name 2 chords.

   _____

5. Travis will skip along 4 arcs. Name 4 arcs.

   _____

   _____

Draw another wrestling mat. Make sure it contains all parts of the circle listed below. Trace them with the colors shown.

     1 center (black)

     2 radii (red)

     2 chords (green)

     2 diameters (orange)

     2 arcs (blue)

Name _____

KEEPING BUSY

Ashley never stops being active in sports! As soon as one season is over, she starts something new. So, she has many labels: athlete, basketball player, volleyball player, tennis player, gymnast, pitcher, and swimmer.

Quadrilaterals are like that, too.
They have many labels.

All quadrilaterals have four sides.
But a four-sided figure can show up
in many "uniforms" or different "looks."

Which figures match each description?
(There may be more than one.)

1. All angles are right angles,
   but all sides are not equal. _____

2. Only one pair of
   opposite sides is parallel. _____

3. A rectangle with
   all sides equal _____

4. A figure with two pairs
   of opposite sides parallel _____

5. A parallelogram with
   all sides the same length _____

6. All sides are equal, but
   all angles may not be equal. _____

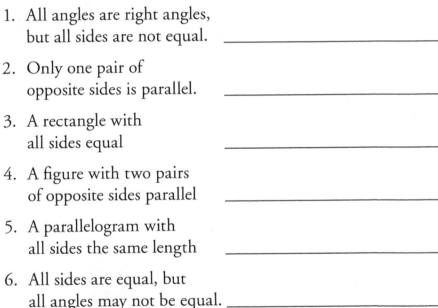

trapezoid
square
quadrilateral
parallelogram
rhombus
rectangle

Write (T) TRUE or (F) FALSE next to each statement.

_____ 1. All squares are rectangles.

_____ 2. All rectangles are quadrilaterals.

_____ 3. No rhombuses are trapezoids.

_____ 4. Rectangles have no right angles.

_____ 5. All rectangles are squares.

_____ 6. A square is a rectangle.

_____ 7. All squares are rhombuses.

_____ 8. A trapezoid is a quadrilateral.

_____ 9. All parallelograms are rectangles.

_____ 10. All rhombuses are squares.

Name _____

Common Core Reinforcement Activities — 4th Grade Math

A CLOSE LOOK AT FIGURES

Wrestlers must get weighed before each match. In wrestling, opponents are matched as closely as possible in size and weight. It doesn't matter if they look similar or have similar figures—it's the exact weight that counts!

Geometric figures that are exactly the same size and shape are congruent with each other. If figures are the same shape, they are similar to each other—no matter what the size.

How would you describe the figures of these two wrestlers? (Circle one answer.)

congruent   similar   neither

Label each pair of figures C (congruent) or S (similar).

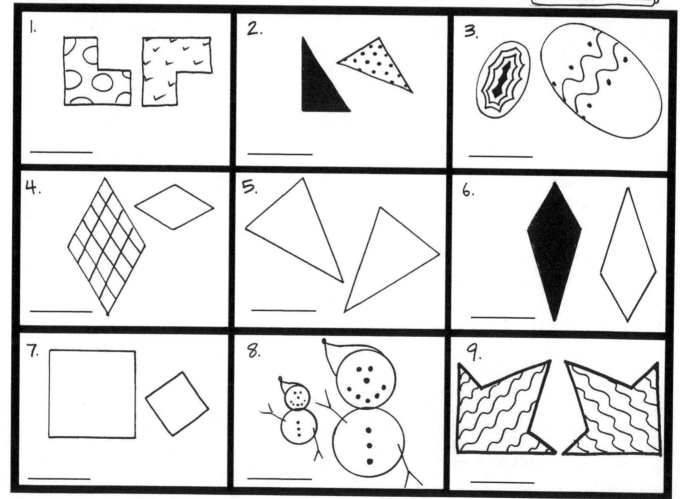

Use with page 123.

Name

A CLOSE LOOK AT FIGURES, continued

A figure is said to be **symmetrical** if it can be cut into two identical (congruent) shapes. The line that cuts the figure is called the **line of symmetry.** It divides the figure into two shapes that are mirror images of each other. The figure can be folded into two matching parts.

A. Draw a line of symmetry to divide this into two congruent shapes.

B. Finish this figure to make it symmetrical. Draw a congruent shape to the bottom of the line of symmetry.

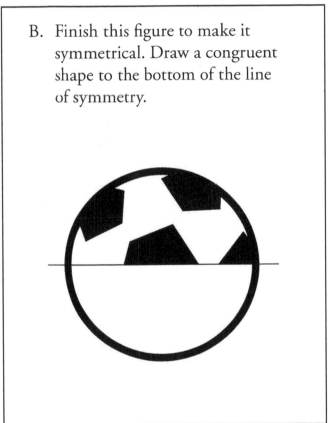

Look back at the figures on page 122. Decide if any of the figures in each item are symmetrical figures. Write *yes* or *no* on the lines below.

_____ 1.   _____ 4.   _____ 7.

_____ 2.   _____ 5.   _____ 8.

_____ 3.   _____ 6.   _____ 9.

Use with page 122.

Name

Common Core Reinforcement Activities — 4th Grade Math

MIRROR IMAGES

Jenna often practices her dance moves in front of a mirror. She hopes the reflection shows a perfect performance.

In a **symmetrical figure**, each half is a perfect reflection of the other.

Look at the figures below. Color the ones that are symmetrical. Use a ruler to draw the line of symmetry in each symmetrical figure.

Complete figures I, J, and K to make them symmetrical. The line of symmetry is already given for you.

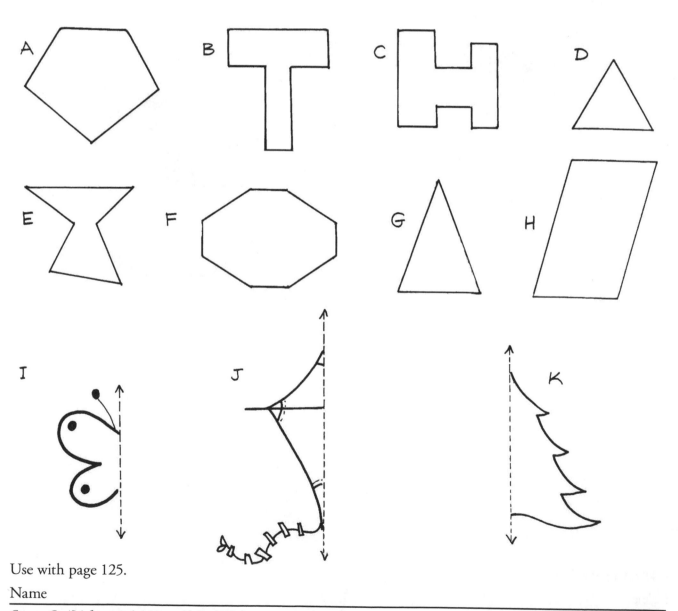

Use with page 125.

Name

MIRROR IMAGES, continued

After you finish page 124, look at these figures. Color any that are **symmetrical**.

Use a ruler to draw the line of symmetry for each symmetrical figure.

Complete figures O, P, and Q to make them symmetrical.

For R, S, and T, draw your own symmetrical figures. Include a line of symmetry.

L

M

N

O

P

Q

R

S

T

Use with page 124.

Name

Common Core Reinforcement Activities — 4th Grade Math

OUT OF ORDER

The sports storage room is a mess. Equipment pieces are out of order. And lots of things are missing!

Look at each item. Decide if it is symmetrical.
Write **yes** or **no** beside the item.

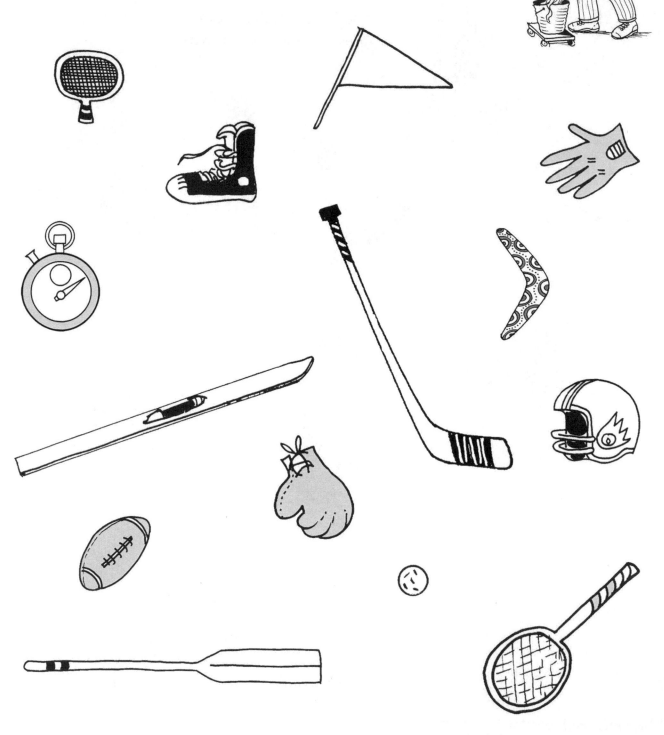

Name

ASSESSMENT
AND
ANSWER KEYS

MATH ASSESSMENT

PART ONE: OPERATIONS AND ALGEBRAIC THINKING

Find the value of n.

1. Frederick lifted 120 kg in his last competition. This was 6 times the weight he lifted in his first competition several years ago. Find the value of **n** to show the weight lifted in his first competition.

    6**n** = 120   **n** = _____ kg

2. Frederick's team traveled 80 km last month. They traveled 4 times that far this month. Find the value of **n** to show how far they have traveled this month.

    n = (80)(4)   **n** = _____ km

Find the value of n.

3. 30 spectators attended the semifinal match. 210 watched the final match.
   How many times more spectators watched the final than the semifinal?

    210 ÷ **n** = 30   **n** = _____

4. Elmo exercised and practiced lifting 84 hours this week. This is 12 times as many hours as he practiced and exercised last week. What was last week's time?

    12**n** = 84   **n** = _____

Answer *yes* or *no*.

5. Last season, the weightlifting team spent $56,000 on hospital visits. The season was 7 months long. The team had 20 members. The coach thinks that $500 was spent each month on each player.

   Is his calculation reasonable? _____

Fill in the blank to finish the statement.

6. 8 times 6 is the same as 6 times _____.

7. _____ times 7 is the same as 7 times 4.

8. _____ x 9 = 9 x 8.

9. 5 x 20 = _____ x 5.

Answer *yes* or *no*.

10. One weightlifter has had 39 sprains or strains so far this season. Eight weeks of the season have passed so far. She tells someone she has had about 8 sprains a week.

    Is this calculation reasonable? _____

11. Yesterday, 200 spectators watched the competition. Today, the number was 50 less than twice yesterday's number. Fran says 150 watched today.

    Is she correct? _____

Name

12. Which numbers on the track are not factors of 28?

Cross them out with an X.

1, 2, 3, 4, 6, 7, 8, 10, 12, 14

13. Which numbers on the track are not factors of 30?

Cross them out with an X.

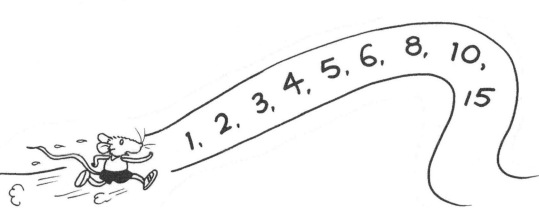

1, 2, 3, 4, 5, 6, 8, 10, 15

14. Circle the common factor of 12 and 15.

2	3	4	5
6	8	9	12

15. Circle common factors of 18 and 30.

2	3	4	5
6	8	9	12

16. Circle multiples of 4.

6	8	72	24
30	66	14	84

17. It takes 3,000 cows to supply enough leather for the footballs used in a year by the National Football League.

Finish the pattern in the numbers below.

3,000	2,965	2,930
_____	2,860	_____

What is the pattern?

_____

_____

_____

Name

Common Core Reinforcement Activities — 4th Grade Math

PART TWO: NUMBER AND OPERATIONS IN BASE TEN

Write <, >, or = in each blank.

1. 32,007 ☐ 32,070

2. 616,066 ☐ 610,660

3. 5,551 ☐ 5,155

Follow the directions.

4. Write a number
   with 60 tens. _____

5. Circle the number
   with 30 thousands.

   3,450   23,059   34,567

6. Circle the number
   with 50 hundreds.

   653   4,505   5,052

7. Round this number
   to the nearest ten: 3,869 _____

8. Round this number
   to the nearest hundred: 64,215 _____

9. 3,214   10. 5,032
   x 2   x 6
   ___   ___

11. 888 − 222 + 333 = _____

12. 567 − 204 = _____

13. 963 ÷ 3 = _____

14. 800 x 4 = _____

Use the numbers on the banners for problems 15–16.

15. What is the number on Banner #1?
    a. eight hundred fifteen thousand, ten
    b. eighty-five thousand, one hundred
    c. eighty-five thousand ten
    d. eight thousand, five hundred, ten

16. What is the number on Banner #2?
    a. two million, two hundred, twenty-two
    b. two hundred twenty-two thousand, two
    c. two hundred twenty thousand, two hundred two
    d. two million, two hundred twenty thousand

Name _____

PART THREE: NUMBER AND OPERATIONS—FRACTIONS

$$\frac{5}{20} \quad \frac{3}{12} \quad \frac{1}{2} \quad \frac{6}{10} \quad \frac{2}{8} \quad \frac{2}{10} \quad \frac{4}{16}$$

1. A basketball player missed one-fourth of the games with a bad case of rat poisoning. Which fractions are equivalent to this amount? Circle them.

Solve the problems.

2. Two-thirds of Elmo's cheese wheel was eaten while he was at basketball practice. Which of these fractions show the amount of the missing cheese? (Circle all answers.)

$$\frac{9}{10} \qquad \frac{4}{6} \qquad \frac{10}{15}$$

$$\frac{6}{9} \qquad \frac{8}{12} \qquad \frac{10}{12}$$

3. After a hard game, Allie drank a half gallon of Thirst Quencher drink. Gigi drank $\frac{6}{7}$ of a gallon.

Who drank more? _____

4. Before the game, the Comets found that $\frac{4}{5}$ of their basketballs were out of air. The Tornados found that $\frac{6}{8}$ of theirs had no air. (Both teams started with 40.)

Which team had **fewer** flat basketballs?

_____

5. These fractions all refer to a part of the same whole. Write them in order from least to greatest.

$$\frac{1}{2} \qquad \frac{3}{4} \qquad \frac{2}{6} \qquad \frac{8}{9} \qquad \frac{7}{12} \qquad \frac{5}{8}$$

_____

Solve the problems. Write answers in lowest terms.

6. In last week's game, $\frac{1}{5}$ of the players got injured. During the week, an additional $\frac{2}{5}$ of the players had some kind of injury. What fraction of the team is now injured? _____

7. $\frac{12}{15} - \frac{4}{15} + \frac{3}{15} - \frac{6}{15} =$ _____

8. $\frac{14}{11} - \frac{6}{11} + \frac{3}{11} +$ _____

9. $50 - 7\frac{4}{5} =$ _____

10. $8\frac{1}{4} - 6\frac{3}{4} =$ _____

11. $\frac{16}{3} + \frac{5}{3} =$ _____

12. $10\frac{5}{6} + \frac{2}{6} =$ _____

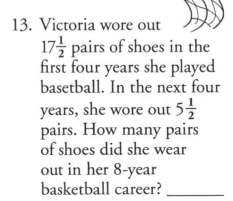

13. Victoria wore out $17\frac{1}{2}$ pairs of shoes in the first four years she played basketball. In the next four years, she wore out $5\frac{1}{2}$ pairs. How many pairs of shoes did she wear out in her 8-year basketball career? _____

Name _____

Common Core Reinforcement Activities — 4th Grade Math

14. The skating pair spent 3 hours practicing their spins and lifts. On Tuesday, they spent $\frac{1}{5}$ the time on spins and lifts.

   How much of Monday's time was spent on spins and lifts? _____

15. $6 \times \frac{2}{4} =$ _____

16. $\frac{2}{9} \times 4 =$ _____

17. $\frac{4}{7} \times 3 =$ _____

Circle one answer.

18. $9 \times \frac{2}{5} =$ _____

   a. $\frac{45}{2}$ c. $\frac{18}{45}$

   b. $\frac{2}{45}$ d. $3\frac{3}{5}$

19. $\frac{1}{8} \times 12 =$ _____

   a. $\frac{8}{12}$ c. $1\frac{1}{2}$

   b. $\frac{1}{96}$ d. $\frac{3}{4}$

20. Is $\frac{4}{5}$ a multiple of $\frac{1}{5}$?

   yes   no

21. **0.36** means

   a. three and six tenths
   b. thirty-six tenths
   c. thirty-six hundredths
   d. thirty-six hundred

22. $\frac{7}{10} = \frac{\boxed{}}{100}$

23. $\frac{4}{10} + \frac{6}{100} = \frac{\boxed{}}{100}$

Write the fractions as decimals.

24. $\frac{3}{10} =$ _____

25. $\frac{54}{100} =$ _____

26. $\frac{19}{100} =$ _____

27. $\frac{5}{10} =$ _____

28. $4\frac{7}{10} =$ _____

29. Gigi's coach used a stopwatch to time her spins. One spin lasted 36.23 seconds. The next spin lasted five hundredths of a second longer.

   How long was the second spin?

   _____

30. Write the names of the skaters in order by their score, from highest to lowest score.

Skaters' Scores	
Winnie	5.97
Minnie	5.77
Millie	5.05
Gigi	5.88
Tina	5.96
Lilly	5.19
Ginni	5.79

   A. _____

   B. _____

   C. _____

   D. _____

   E. _____

   F. _____

   G. _____

Name

PART FOUR: MEASUREMENT AND DATA

Write the correct amount.

1. The track team traveled 6 hr. This is _____ min.

2. A bag of team snacks weighs 1,000 g. This is _____ kg.

3. The hurdler fell 10 yd from the finish line. This is _____ ft.

4. Lottie was 10,000 cm from the finish line. This is _____ m.

5. Fans drank 40,000 mL of coffee. This is _____ L.

6. The vaulter jumped a 16-foot height. This is _____ in.

7. The next track meet will be held in 9 weeks. This is _____ hr.

8. The marathon runner passed 26 miles. This is _____ ft.

Solve the problems.

9. The long jump competition just ended at 3:25 p.m. after 2 hr, 40 min.

   What time did it begin? _____

10. Gregorio ran 15.5 km today. Lucy ran 13,620 m.

    What was the difference between their distances? _____

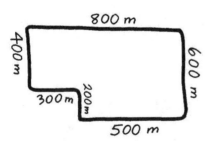

11. Max jogs around this field twice a day. How far does he run?

    _____

Solve the problems.

12. Felix's gold medal weighs 7.3 g. He has three of them. What is the total weight? _____

13. The diameter of the medal is 7 cm. What is its circumference? _____

14. After track practice, Alexa dives into a pool to cool off. The rectangular pool is 510 yd wide and 950 yd long. What is the area of the water surface? _____

15. The pole vault pit is 67 by 129 in. What is the area of its surface?

    _____

16. The area of a rectangular storage closet at Bud's gym is 54 ft². The width of the closet is 6 ft. What is its length?

    _____

Name _____

Common Core Reinforcement Activities — 4th Grade Math

Hockey Falls—Tournament Data

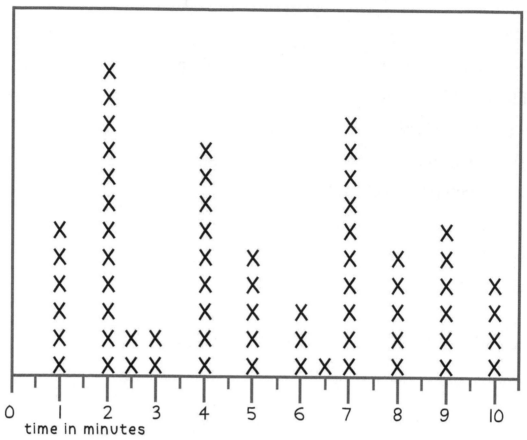

time in minutes

The assistant hockey coach kept track of the total number of minutes each player spent sprawled on the ice during the final two games of the tournament. Each X represents one player. Use the line plot to answer questions 17 and 18.

17. How many players are represented by the data? ____

18. What was the most frequent time spent fallen? ____

19. How many players spent more than 7 minutes down? ____

20. How many players were
    down less than one minute? ____

21. How many players were
    down less than 5 minutes? ____

22. Which span of time covers the most players:
    >4 and <7   or   <9 and >6?
    (Circle one.)

Name ____

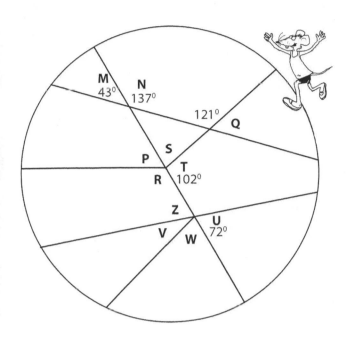

Use the diagram to answer questions 23–26.

23. Would angle R be closer
    in measure to 100°, 75°,
    or 155°?   _____°

24. If angle W measures 73°,
    what is angle V's measure?   _____°

25. What is the measurement
    of angle S?   _____°

26. What is the measurement
    of the other two angles
    in the same triangle
    with angle S?   _____° and _____°

**Draw an angle that matches each
measurement. Do not use a protractor.
Do your best to draw an estimate.**

27. 300°

28. 35°

29. 160°

30. 125°

PART FIVE: GEOMETRY

Read the label on each sign.

Draw a figure to match the label.

1. line

2. line segment

3. point

4. ray

5. parallel lines

6. right angle

7. acute angle

8. obtuse angle

9. straight angle

10. intersecting line segments

Name

Write T for true and F for false.

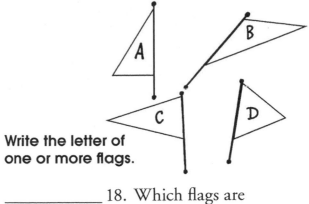

_____ 11. All rectangles have four right angles.

_____ 12. A square has two pairs of parallel lines.

_____ 13. A trapezoid has two pairs
of parallel lines.

_____ 14. A triangle has no parallel lines.

_____ 15. An equilateral triangle
has no acute angles.

_____ 16. A right triangle has
perpendicular lines.

_____ 17. An isosceles triangle
can have an obtuse angle.

**Write the letter of
one or more flags.**

_____ 18. Which flags are
equilateral triangles?

_____ 19. Which flags are
right triangles?

_____ 20. Which flags are
isosceles triangles?

21. Circle the letters of symmetrical figures. Draw a line of symmetry for any symmetrical figure.

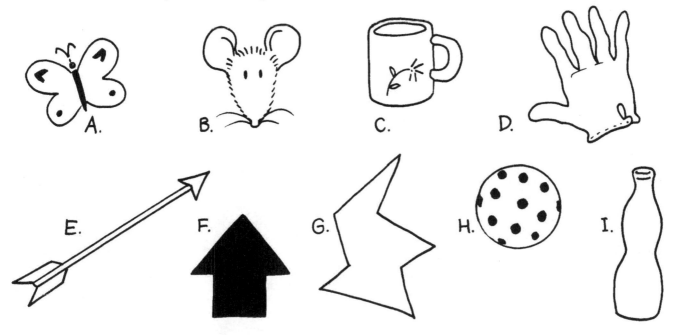

22. Draw two symmetrical figures of your choice. Add the line of symmetry for each figure.

Name

Common Core Reinforcement Activities — 4th Grade Math

ASSESSMENT ANSWER KEY

Part One: Operations and Algebraic Thinking

1. 20
2. 320
3. 7
4. 7
5. no

6. 8
7. 4
8. 8
9. 20
10. no

11. no
12. 3, 6, 8, 10, 12
13. 4, 8
14. 3
15. 2, 3, 6

16. 8, 24, 72, 84
17. 2, 895; 2, 825; pattern is subtract 35

Part Two: Number and Operations in Base Ten

1. <
2. >
3. >
4. Answers will vary.

5. 34,567
6. 5,052
7. 3,870
8. 64,200

9. 6,428
10. 30,192
11. 999
12. 363

13. 321
14. 3,200
15. b
16. c

Part Three: Number and Operations: Fractions

1. Circle: $\frac{5}{20}$; $\frac{3}{12}$; $\frac{2}{8}$; $\frac{4}{16}$
2. $\frac{4}{6}$, $\frac{6}{9}$, $\frac{8}{12}$, $\frac{10}{15}$
3. Gigi
4. Tornados
5. $\frac{2}{6}$; $\frac{1}{2}$; $\frac{7}{12}$; $\frac{5}{8}$; $\frac{3}{4}$; $\frac{8}{9}$
6. $\frac{3}{5}$
7. $\frac{5}{15}$ $\left(\frac{1}{3}\right)$
8. $\frac{5}{11}$

9. $42\frac{1}{5}$
10. $1\frac{2}{4}$ $\left(1\frac{1}{2}\right)$
11. $\frac{21}{3}$ (7)
12. $11\frac{1}{6}$
13. 23
14. $\frac{3}{5}$ hour (36 minutes)
15. $\frac{12}{4}$ (3)

16. $\frac{8}{9}$
17. $\frac{12}{7}$ (or $1\frac{5}{7}$)
18. d
19. c
20. yes
21. c
22. 70
23. 46
24. 0.3

25. 0.54
26. 0.19
27. 0.5
28. 4.7
29. 36.28
30. A. Winnie
    B. Tina
    C. Gigi
    D. Ginni
    E. Minnie
    F. Lilly
    G. Millie

Part Four: Measurement and Data

1. 360
2. 1
3. 30
4. 100
5. 40
6. 192
7. 1,512
8. 137,280

9. 12:45 p.m.
10. 1,880 m
11. 5,600 m
12. 21.9 g
13. 21.98 cm
14. 484,500 yd^2
15. 8,643 in^2
16. 9 ft

17. 65
18. 2 min
19. 15
20. 0
21. 31
22. < 9 and > 6
23. 100°
24. 35°

25. 78°
26. 59° and 43°
27-30: Examine angles to see that they approximate the measurements.

Part Five: Geometry

1-10: Examine drawings to see that they match the figure names.
11. T
12. T
13. F

14. T
15. F
16. T
17. T
18. D
19. A

20. B. C
21. A, B, E, F, H, I (C could be symmetrical if cut in center of handle.) Check for lines of symmetry drawn accurately.

22. Check drawings to see that they approximate symmetrical and that lines of symmetry are included.

ACTIVITIES ANSWER KEY

Operations and Algebraic Thinking (pages 18–34)

Page 18
1. 32
2. 54
3. 24
4. 6, 6
5. 63
6. 28, 4
7. 45
8. 8, 8

Page 19
1. 9 x 8 = 72
   (or 8 x 9 = 72)
2. 5 x 7 = 35
3. 6 x 10 = 60
4. 7 x 2 = 14
5. 9 x 3 = 27
6. 4 x 10 = 40
7. 6 x 4 = 24
8. 6 x 5 = 30

Pages 20–21
1. c; n = 100
2. a; n = 12 feet
3. b; n = 6
4. a; n = 30°F
5. n x 2 = 220
   (or 2 x n = 220);
   n = 110 seconds
6. 260 ÷ 20 = n
   (or 260 ÷ n = 20);
   n = 13
7. 480 ÷ n = 24
   (or 480 ÷ 24 = n);
   n = 20
8. n x 3 = 150
   (or 3 x n = 150);
   n = 50

Page 22
1. n = 3
2. n = 1,200
3. n = 4
4. n = 12
5. 110
6. 3

Page 23
1. n = 2
2. n = 8
3. n = 12
4. n = 50
5. n = $650
6. n = 792
7. n = 8

Page 24
1. $3
2. 90 ft
3. $7 each
4. 3
5. 4
6. $300

Page 25
1. b; n = 5
2. a; n = 63
3. b; n = 32 miles
4. c; n = 2,870
5. c; n = 1,000 ft

Page 26
1. yes
2. no
3. no
4. yes
5. yes

Page 27
1. no
2. no
3. no
4. yes
5. yes
6. yes
7. no
8. no
9. no
10. yes

Page 28
1. yes
2. no
3. no
4. no
5. yes
6. no
7. no
8. yes
9. yes
10. yes

Page 29
Answers will vary some. Check to make sure factors listed are among those shown below. Note those that are prime.
1. 18: 1, 2, 3, 6, 9, 18
   (primes: 2, 3)
2. 10: 1, 2, 5, 10
   (primes 2, 5)
3. 15: 1, 3, 5, 15
   (primes: 3, 5)
4. 45: 1, 3, 5, 9, 15, 45
   (primes: 3, 5)
5. 6: 1, 2, 3, 6
   (primes: 2, 3)
6. 90: 1, 2, 3, 5, 6, 9, 10, 15, 18, 30, 45, 90
   (primes: 2, 3, 5)
7. 21: 1, 3, 7, 21
   (primes: 3, 7)
8. 33: 1, 3, 11, 33
   (primes 3, 11)
9. 24: 1, 2, 3, 4, 6, 8, 12, 24
   (primes: 2, 3)
10. 56: 1, 2, 4, 7, 8, 14, 28, 56 (primes: 2, 7)
11. 32: 1, 2, 4, 8, 16, 32
    (primes: 2)
12. 27: 1, 3, 9, 27
    (primes: 3)
13. 42: 1, 2, 3, 6, 7, 14, 21, 42
    (primes: 2, 3, 7)
14. 40: 1, 2, 4, 5, 8, 10, 20, 40 (primes: 2, 5)
15. 39: 1, 3, 13, 39
    (primes: 3, 13, 39)

Page 30
1. 2	15. 2
2. 3	16. 10
3. 11	17. 5
4. 14	18. 5
5. 15	19. 4
6. 6	20. 7
7. 4	21. 4
8. 3	22. 10
9. 10	23. 5
10. 12	24. 10
11. 3	25. 2
12. 4	26. 3
13. 2	27. 3
14. 2	

Puzzle Solution: The driver dragged a garden rake.

Page 31
1. l, m
2. c
3. none
4. b, j, k, m
5. h
6. a, b, c
7. one
8. j

Page 32
1. fifth minute
2. subtract 30
3. 360
4. 48 minutes
5. Pattern is: 820, 780, 740, 700, 660, 620, 580, 540, 500, 460
6. Add 25, then double the number added each hour.

Page 33
Completed chart should read:
1. Lance: 7, 10, 13, 16, 19, 22
2. Fran: 1, 2, 4, 8, 16, 32
3. Sam: 41, 39, 37, 35, 33, 31
4. Vance: 25, 25, 25, 25, 25, 25
5. Stan: 3, 6, 10, 15, 21, 28
6. Pam: 8, 10, 12, 15, 18, 21
7. Nan: 18, 17, 15, 12, 8, 3

Page 34
1. 187 pounds
2. 180 kg
3. missing numbers: 946, 7,568; pattern is *multiply by 2*
4. missing number: 20; pattern is *divide by 10*
5. missing number: 255 (pattern is *double the number plus 1*)
6. missing number: 160; pattern is *divide by 5*
7. 13 (pattern is *add 3*)
8. missing numbers: 80, 90 (pattern is *add 8, add 2*)

Number and Operations in Base Ten (pages 36–54)

Pages 36–37
1. 11,028
2. 43,000,000,000
3. 50
4. 50
5. four billion, three hundred million
6. <
7. 10
8. 29,228
9. 3,000,000,000
10. 20
11. 50
12. 400
13. 147
14. 10
15. 61,600; <
16. one thousand, nine hundred, thirty-three
17. 1,300,000; >
18. 1

Page 38
Down
1. 40,973
2. 151,600
3. 900,901
7. 71,800,003
8. 610,390
9. 450,009
Across
4. 300,050,008
5. 2,600,900
6. 207
10. 12,008,035
11. 8,351
12. 909
13. 300,300

Page 39
1. Numbers from top to bottom should read: 11, 7, 8, 2, 6, 4, 9, 5, 3, 10, 1, 12
2. Numbers from top to bottom should read: 5, 4, 6, 2, 1, 9, 7, 3, 8

Page 40
1. 338
2. 33
3. 250, 271, or 1,271
4. 3,000
5. 90
6. 69

7. 271
8. 128
9. 491
10. 474
11. 1,272
12. 5,010

Page 41

Blue	Yellow
1. 60	20. 50
2. 2,200	21. 6,000
3. 8	**Purple**
4. 100	22. 800
5. 72,000	23. 8,000
6. 9,000	24. 6
7. 80	25. 70,000
8. 45,000	26. 20
9. 600	27. 300
10. 112	28. 170
11. 700	29. 16
12. 48	**Orange**
Red	30. 1,200
13. 12,000	31. 4,800
14. 70	**Green**
White	22, 5, 7,
15. 9	11, 2, 15,
16. 20,000	30, 12, 1,
17. 14	40, 10
18. 4	
19. 3	

Page 42

1. 11,000	13. 61,000
2. 270	14. 775,000
3. 2,000	15. 10,990
4. 360	16. 770
5. 900	17. 98,900
6. 7,490	18. 610
7. 15,000	19. 600
8. 5,000	20. 56,000
9. 800,400	21. 900
10. 750,000	22. 20,000
11. 1,000,000	23. 600,000
12. 101,330	24. 1,510

Page 43

1. 380	9. 503,210
2. 900	10. 400,000
3. 7,490	11. 760
4. 15,000	12. 800
5. 4,000	13. 9,900
6. 80,100	14. 610
7. 750,000	15. 600
8. 100,000	

Page 44
1. 2,000
2. 48,580
3. 260
4. 80
5. 3,000
6. 1,100
7. 660,000
8. 300,000,000

Page 45
1. 11,158
2. 1,129
3. Germany
4. 2,741
5. Argentina
6. 3,086
7. 271
8. Switzerland
9. 17
10. 15

Page 46

1. 271	8. 5,297
2. 217	9. 3,702
3. 14	10. 581
4. 42	11. 5,654
5. 274	12. 7,275
6. 35	13. 721,320
7. 407	14. 12,138

Page 47

1. 56	9. 515
2. 312	10. 873
3. 522	11. 125,649
4. 940	12. 11,038
5. 113	13. 7,495
6. 111	14. 2,062
7. 1,254	15. 2,892
8. 189	16. 7,358

Page 48
Answer to problem in illustration = 100.

1. 170	5. 60
2. 500	6. 1,999
3. 999	7. 2,030
4. 877	8. 9,000

Page 49
1. 3,672
2. 506
3. 675

4. Blanks: 40,000; 0; 150; 20; Answer: 40,170
5. Blanks: 3,000, 300, 48; Answer: 3,348
6. Blanks: 2,400; 60; 480; 12; Answer: 2,952
7. Blanks: 18,000; 1,500; 120; 9; Answer: 19,629
8. Blanks: 3,600; 280; 16; Answer: 3,896
9. Blanks: 600; 90; 480; 72; Answer: 1,242

Page 50
Check colored pictures to see that correct answers match colors.

Page 51

1. 230	11. 440
2. 2,300	12. 44
3. 930	13. 22
4. 111,000	14. 100
5. 5,050	15. 10
6. 888,800	16. 33
7. 7,170,000	17. 880
8. 80,480	18. 10
9. 2,800	19. 70
10. 250,000	20. 6,107

Page 52

1. £95	5. £90
2. 1,625,000	6. 109
3. £500	7. £28
4. 109	8. £150

Page 53

1. 700	8. 200
2. 300	9. 4,000
3. 950	10. 1,300
4. 200	11. 910
5. 1,460	12. 409
6. 1,000	13. 1,589
7. 1,700	14. 5,791

Page 54
1. Circles colored red: 1, 8, 160, 80; Trophy: 92
2. Circles colored green: 2, 26, 106, 212; Trophy: 200
3. Circles colored purple: 3, 45, 5, 55; Trophy: 11
4. Circles colored blue: 4, 84, 74, 174; Trophy: 0

Number and Operations—Fractions (pages 56–84)

Page 56

1–4: Explanations may vary. Student may say that the numerator and denominator of one fraction have been multiplied by the same number to get the second fraction.

5–10: Equivalent fractions may vary. Here are some possibilities:

5. $\frac{2}{18}$

6. $\frac{2}{3}$

7. $\frac{2}{5}$

8. $\frac{1}{1}$

9. $\frac{4}{10}$

10. $\frac{2}{16}$

Page 57

1. $\frac{5}{9}$ 140 mph

2. $\frac{1}{5}$ ice hockey

3. $\frac{7}{9}$ 130 mph

4. $\frac{3}{5}$ 1 or 2

5. $\frac{5}{8}$ 1998

6. $\frac{9}{12}$ Viking ship

7. $\frac{1}{11}$ 9,000 years

8. $\frac{3}{4}$ about 800 feet

9. $\frac{5}{11}$ cross-country skiing and rifle shooting

10. $\frac{2}{6}$ quadruple salchow

Page 58

1. $< (\frac{10}{20} < \frac{12}{20})$

2. $> (\frac{4}{6} > \frac{2}{6})$

3. $= (\frac{4}{8} = \frac{4}{8})$

4. $< (\frac{6}{21} < \frac{7}{21})$

5. $> (\frac{2}{6} > \frac{1}{6})$

6. $> (\frac{5}{6} > \frac{2}{6})$

7. $< (\frac{6}{8} < \frac{7}{8})$

8. $= (\frac{4}{10} = \frac{4}{10})$

9. $< (\frac{15}{24} < \frac{16}{24})$

10. $< (\frac{28}{36} < \frac{33}{36})$

11. $< (\frac{6}{30} < \frac{25}{30})$

12. $= (\frac{2}{10} = \frac{2}{10})$

13. $\frac{1}{4}, \frac{2}{5}, \frac{1}{2}$

14. $\frac{3}{18}, \frac{2}{3}, \frac{5}{6}$

15. $\frac{2}{5}, \frac{5}{10}, \frac{6}{8}$

Page 59

Path follows these statements:

$\frac{8}{12} = \frac{2}{3}$; $\frac{2}{4} = \frac{5}{10}$;

$\frac{6}{3} = \frac{8}{4}$; $\frac{8}{4} = \frac{12}{6}$;

$\frac{20}{25} = \frac{4}{5}$; $\frac{7}{12} = \frac{14}{24}$;

$\frac{1}{2} > \frac{2}{5}$; $\frac{2}{3} = \frac{4}{6}$

Page 60

1. $\frac{5}{6}$ (green)

2. $\frac{3}{10}$ (red)

3. $\frac{1}{12}$ (blue)

4. $\frac{1}{8}$ (yellow)

5. $\frac{1}{2}$ (purple)

6. $\frac{4}{5}$ (brown)

7. $\frac{1}{6}$ (orange)

8. $\frac{13}{22}$ (pink)

9. $\frac{1}{3}$ (red)

10. $\frac{4}{9}$ (blue)

11. $\frac{7}{9}$ (purple)

12. $\frac{19}{21}$ (green)

13. $\frac{1}{2}$ (orange)

14. $\frac{19}{24}$ (brown)

Page 61

1. $1\frac{9}{10}$

2. $\frac{2}{3}$

3. $\frac{7}{13}$

4. $\frac{2}{3}$

5. $\frac{3}{4}$

6. $\frac{6}{11}$

7. 1

8. $\frac{15}{16}$

9. $\frac{2}{5}$

10. $\frac{1}{6}$

11. $4\frac{5}{6}$

12. $\frac{71}{100}$

Page 62

Top

1. K   5. DS
2. AT   6. I
3. SPE   7. E
4. G   8. N

Answer: SPEED SKATING

Bottom:

1. N   4. L
2. L   5. D
3. OW   6. HI

Answer: DOWNHILL

Page 63

1. $\frac{57}{2} = 28\frac{1}{2}$

2. $\frac{59}{6} = 9\frac{5}{6}$

3. $\frac{97}{4} = 24\frac{1}{4}$

4. $\frac{47}{2} = 23\frac{1}{2}$

5. $\frac{32}{5} = 6\frac{2}{5}$

6. $\frac{87}{8} = 10\frac{7}{8}$

7. $\frac{88}{3} = 29\frac{1}{3}$

8. $\frac{49}{4} = 12\frac{1}{4}$

9. $\frac{109}{4} = 27\frac{1}{4}$

10. $\frac{71}{3} = 23\frac{2}{3}$

11. $\frac{73}{5} = 14\frac{3}{5}$

12. $\frac{165}{5} = 33$

Page 64

The shell on the right is a scull.

1. $11\frac{3}{4}$

2. $26\frac{5}{8}$

3. $17\frac{2}{5}$

4. $10\frac{1}{4}$

5. 12

6. 3

7. 11

8. 10

9. $1\frac{1}{5}$

10. $10\frac{1}{11}$

11. $6\frac{4}{9}$

12. $19\frac{4}{5}$

13. 25

14. $15\frac{1}{6}$

15. 6

Page 65

1. $\frac{4}{4} = 1$

2. $\frac{3}{3} = 1$

3. $\frac{5}{4} = 1\frac{1}{4}$

4. $\frac{5}{12}$

5. $\frac{5}{12}$

6. $\frac{11}{12}$

7. $9\frac{4}{5}$

8. $3\frac{9}{10}$

9. $10\frac{1}{2}$

10. 23

Page 66

1. $\frac{4}{10} + \frac{9}{10} = 1\frac{3}{10}$

2. $\frac{6}{20} - \frac{2}{20} = \frac{4}{20} = \frac{2}{10} = \frac{1}{5}$

3. $\frac{20}{20} - \frac{7}{20} = \frac{13}{20}$

4. $1 - \frac{4}{10} - \frac{1}{10} = \frac{5}{10} = \frac{1}{2}$

5. $\frac{9}{20}$

6. $1 - \frac{3}{9} - \frac{4}{9} = \frac{2}{9}$

7. $1 - \frac{2}{5} - \frac{5}{10} = $
   $1 - \frac{4}{10} - \frac{5}{10} = \frac{1}{10}$

Page 67

1. $4\frac{2}{3}$ cups

2. $\frac{3}{4}$ teaspoon

3. $\frac{4}{3}$ or $1\frac{1}{3}$ cups

4. 6

5. $\frac{2}{5}$

6. $2\frac{1}{4}$ cups

Page 68

1. c   3. a   5. b   7. c
2. b   4. a   6. b

Common Core Reinforcement Activities — 4th Grade Math

Page 69

The following statements are true and thus these sections of the track should be colored: 2, 3, 4, 8, 9, 10, 15

Page 70

1. RED: $\frac{2}{7}$; $\frac{3}{7}$; $\frac{4}{7}$
2. BLUE: $\frac{2}{9}$; $\frac{4}{9}$; $\frac{6}{9}$
3. GREEN: $\frac{6}{8}$; $\frac{4}{8}$; $\frac{7}{8}$
4. YELLOW: $\frac{12}{15}$; $\frac{6}{15}$
5. PURPLE: $\frac{12}{22}$
6. ORANGE: $\frac{3}{20}$
7. PINK: $\frac{9}{12}$
8. BROWN: $\frac{20}{25}$

Page 71

1. no	5. no	9. yes
2. no	6. yes	10. yes
3. yes	7. no	11. yes
4. yes	8. no	12. yes

Page 72

New Recipe:

11 pounds potatoes

$16\frac{1}{2}$ quarts boiling water

4 large onions

$16\frac{1}{4}$ cups chicken broth

$9\frac{1}{3}$ carrots, chopped

17 celery sticks, sliced

3 green peppers, chopped

$10\frac{2}{3}$ cups frozen corn

$9\frac{1}{2}$ pounds mushrooms

$14\frac{1}{2}$ cups cooked chicken, diced

$6\frac{2}{3}$ teaspoons salt

$12\frac{2}{3}$ Tablespoons mixed herbs

Page 73

1. $\frac{22}{10}$
2. $\frac{10}{22}$
3. $\frac{14}{7}$
4. $\frac{12}{30}$
5. $\frac{4}{3}$

6. $\frac{6}{15}$
7. $\frac{21}{5}$
8. $\frac{9}{11}$
9. $\frac{10}{25}$
10. $\frac{8}{10}$
11. $\frac{15}{100}$
12. $\frac{6}{14}$

Page 74

1. $68\frac{1}{4}$ miles
2. $61\frac{1}{2}$ minutes
3. $1\frac{1}{2}$ hours
4. $14\frac{2}{3}$
5. 7 minutes
6. $8\frac{1}{2}$ hours
7. $33\frac{3}{4}$ minutes
8. $5\frac{1}{2}$ pizzas

Page 75

1. 4
2. 72
3. 18
4. 81 miles
5. 15
6. 24
7. 36
8. 25

Page 76

1. $n = 4\frac{3}{8}$
2. $n = 6$
3. $n = 2\frac{1}{3}$
4. $n = 48$
5. $n = 2\frac{2}{5}$
6. $4\frac{1}{2}$

Page 77

2. $\frac{89}{100}$
3. $\frac{73}{100}$
4. $\frac{48}{100}$
5. $\frac{90}{100}$
6. $\frac{52}{100}$
7. $\frac{77}{100}$
8. $\frac{66}{100}$

Page 78

Decimals:

Magic:	.85
Christian:	.63
Clyde:	.83
David:	.54
Charles:	.85
Michael:	.75
Karl:	.59
Patrick:	.63
Larry:	.75
John:	.50
Chris:	.64
Scottie:	.68

1. John's
2. two
3. Magic and Charles; Michael and Larry; Christian and Patrick
4. Scottie
5. Chris
6. $\frac{24}{100}$ or twenty-four hundredths

Page 79

1. 0.75	8. 9.9
2. 7.5	9. 5.07
3. 0.55	10. 55.5
4. 500.05	11. 9.99
5. 75	12. 11.6
6. 0.90	13. 1.16
7. 0.05	14. 0.16

Page 80

Order of numbers, from top of left column to bottom of right.

Trick # 1: 2, 1, 5, 7, 4, 6, 8, 3

Trick # 2: 6, 3, 1, 2, 7, 4, 8, 5

Trick # 3: 6, 4, 3, 1, 7, 8, 5, 2

Trick # 4: 5, 8, 3, 4, 6, 1, 7, 2

Trick # 5: 2, 3, 1, 8, 6, 4, 7, 5

Trick # 6: 5, 4, 3, 7, 6, 8, 2, 1

Trick # 7: 2, 4, 8, 6, 1, 5, 7, 3

Page 81

1. <	6. >	11. >
2. =	7. =	12. =
3. >	8. <	13. <
4. <	9. >	14. <
5. <	10. <	15. =

Page 82

1. Karin: 39.479—4th
2. Sofia: 39.272—5th

3. Elena: 37.901—11th
4. Kim: 38.464—9th
5. Kerri: 38.886—6th
6. Tatiana: 39.928—1st
7. Nina: 38.562—7th
8. Larissa: 38.545—8th
9. Svetlana: 39.738—2nd
10. Olga: 37.063—12th
11. Kathy: 39.482—3rd
12. Tamara: 38.289—10th

Gold—Tatiana;
Silver—Svetlana;
Bronze—Kathy

Page 83

1. Red: 7.1
2. Blue: 6.35
3. Pink: 0.6
4. Black: 100.12
5. Yellow: 0.36
6. Purple: 0.09
7. Tan: 9.1
8. Orange: 14.2
9. Brown: 2.05
10. Tan: 0.9
11. Silver: 0.24
12. Green: 0.99
13. Red: 10.12
14. Blue: 8.08
15. Green: 9.9
16. Pink: 8.8
17. Purple: 2.4
18. Red: 0.009
19. Orange: 0.22
20. Yellow: 3.6
21. Blue: 0.5
22. Green: 50.5
23. Silver: 20.5
24. Purple: 100.2

Page 84

Path on top half of net:

Player to 0.62—0.65—0.71—0.91—0.93—1.1—1.3—1.31—1.4—1.44—1.62—1.7—1.77—1.78

Path on bottom half of net:

Player to 0.11—0.15—0.64—0.71—0.9—1.3—1.33—1.6—1.7—1.75—1.9—2.1—2.11—2.3

Measurement and Data (Pages 86–110)

Page 86

1. =	11. >
2. =	12. >
3. >	13. >
4. =	14. >
5. =	15. <
6. <	16. <
7. =	17. >
8. >	18. <
9. =	19. =
10. =	20. =

Page 87

1. no
2. yes
3. yes
4. no
5. no
6. no
7. no
8. yes
9. yes
10. neither: 68 km = 6,800 meters and 680,000 centimeters

Page 88

1. wrong; liters (or kiloliters, milliliters, deciliters); OR teaspoons, tablespoons, cups, pints, quarts, or gallons
2. correct
3. correct
4. correct
5. wrong; 2 kilometers
6. correct
7. correct
8. wrong; 1,000
9. wrong; 1,000
10. correct
11. wrong; 2,000
12. correct
13. correct
14. wrong; 1,000
15. wrong; 10,000
16. correct
   No, Tom will not pass.

Page 89

1. 24	7. 3,000
2. 5,280	8. 30,000
3. 8	9. 1,700
4. 32	10. 16
5. 300	11. 17,000
6. 36	12. 63

Page 90

Matching pairs:

1 & 15	7 & 9
2 & 17	8 & 10
3 & 11	13 & 16
4 & 5	14 & 20
6 & 12	18 & 19

Page 91

1. a	5. c
2. b	6. b
3. a	7. b
4. c	8. b

Page 92

1. 30 gal
2. 17
3. 80
4. 130 g
5. 3
6. $90
7. $1\frac{1}{2}$ hr
8. $3,700
9. 15,000,000 m

Page 93

1. no	7. no
2. yes	8. no
3. yes	9. yes
4. no	10. yes
5. no	11. yes
6. yes	

Pages 94–95

1. Baseball field:
   P = 360 feet;
   A = 8,100 feet^2
2. Boxing Ring:
   P = 64 feet;
   A = 256 feet^2
3. Swimming Pool:
   P = 604 feet;
   A = 14,880 feet^2
4. Tennis Court:
   P = 228 feet;
   A = 2,808 feet^2
5. Archery Range:
   P = 180 feet;
   A = 1,125 feet^2
6. Sailboat:
   A = 207 feet^2
7. Wrestling Mat:
   P = 75.36 feet;
   A = 452.16 feet^2
8. Track:
   P = 1,828 feet;
   A = 151,400 feet^2

Page 96

1. energy bar:
   A = 10 in^2
2. towel:
   A = 1,500 cm^2;
   P = 160 cm
3. magazine:
   A = 140 in^2
4. box top: P = 18 in
5. cap: P = 25.12 in
6. tennis ball can:
   A = 28.26 in^2
7. soap: A = 9 in^2
8. Thirst Quench:
   A = 200.96 cm^2

Page 97

Check line plot to see that there are the following number of X's:

1: 3	4: 4
2: 5	5: 6
3: 3	5.5: 1
3.5: 1	6: 4

Page 98

1. 11
2. 15
3. 2 and 8 seconds
4. 60
5. 37
6. Answers will vary: Fewer walls lasted the shortest and longest times. More walls fell in the middle times, 4–7 seconds.

Page 99

1. 9	4. 31
2. 11	5. 65
3. 26	6. 18

Page 100

1. 44	4. none
2. 65 ft	5. > 30 < 65
3. 19	

Page 101

Check to see that appropriate numbers of X's are shown at proper locations.

Pages 102–103

A.	45°		or 200°
B.	30°	H.	180°
C.	60°	I.	25°
D.	110°	J.	250°
E.	75°	K.	150°
F.	90°	L.	325°
G.	195°		

Page 104

1.	90°	5.	95°
2.	20°	6.	150°
3.	110°	7.	35°
4.	80°	8.	65°

Page 105

Angle measurements may vary some. Allow answers close to these.

1. 55°
2. both angles are 90°
3. 80°
4. angle on left is 65°; on right is 115°
5. angle on left is 60°; on right is 130°
6. 110°
7. 240°
8. angle below leg is 130°; above leg is 50°

Pages 106–107

Angle measurements may vary some. Allow answers close to these.

1.	180°	5.	180°
2.	180°	6.	30°
3.	90°	7.	210°
4.	180°	8.	360°

Page 108

Angle measurements may vary some. Allow answers close to these.

1. 90°
2. 130°
3. 50°
4. 270°

5. 100°
6. 210°
7. 50°
8. 270°
9. 310°
10. 45°

Pages 109–110

1. 140°
2. 40°
3. 16°
4. 170°
5. 180°
6. 180°
7. 42°
8. 360°
9. 180°
10. 59°
11. 180°
12. 78°
13. 360°
14. 180°
15. 73°
16. 180°

Geometry (pages 112–126)

Page 112

1. Plane ABCD
2. Ray AB
3. Line Segment AB
4. Point B
5. Line AB
6. Angle ABC
7. Angle CBD
8. Angle ACB
9. Line Segment BC
10. Angle DCE

Page 113

Answers may vary some. Here are several. Students may find more.

1. 13 (or 15) in the figure—more in the letters PS, PM, PQ, SM, MQ, SQ, QT, TR, RN, NU, RO, OU, NO
2. 36: SMP, SPM, SPQ, PMQ, PQM, QSP, PQS, SQT, QTS, TSQ, QTR, TRQ, TQR, TRU, RUT, RNO, UNO, UON, RON, ONU, ONR, PQT, QTS, TSP, SPQ, QRU, RUT, UTQ, TQR, TRO, ROU, OUT, UTR
3. Check to see that this is done in the right location.

Page 114

Check to see that students have traced three of each figure.

Page 115

1. D
2. C
3. A
4. F

5. B
6. E
7. G

8–10. Check drawings for accuracy.

Page 116

1. F, K, Q
2. B, C, H, J, L
3. A E, G, P, O

Page 117

Check designs for accurate coloring.

Page 118

A. octagon
B. hexagon
C. pentagon
D. trapezoid
E. square
F. rectangle (or square)
G. parallelogram, rectangle, or square
H. quadrilateral
I. obtuse triangle
J. equilateral triangle
K. right triangle
L. scalene triangle
M. triangle
N. polygon
O. isosceles triangle
P. rhombus (or square)

Page 119

Check designs for accurate coloring. Item is an arrow; sport is archery.

Page 120

1. N
2. TQ (or QT) and MK (or KM)

3. NH (or HN), NT (or TN), NQ (or QN), NK (or KN), NM (or MN)
4. QJ (or JQ), RS (or SR)
5. HT (or TH), TJ (or JT), JK (or KJ), KQ (or QK), QS (or SQ), SR (or RS), RM (or MR), MH (or HM)

Check drawings for accuracy.

Page 121

1. rectangle
2. trapezoid
3. square
4. parallelogram, square, or rectangle
5. rhombus or square
6. rhombus

Bottom:

1. T
2. T
3. T
4. F
5. F
6. T
7. T
8. T
9. F
10. F

Page 122

The wrestler's figures are similar.

1. C
2. C
3. S
4. S
5. C
6. C
7. S
8. S
9. C

Page 123

A and B—Check drawings for accurate line of symmetry and accurate drawings.

1. yes (diagonal)
2. no
3. yes
4. yes
5. yes
6. yes
7. yes
8. no
9. yes (diagonal)

Pages 124–125

Figures A, B, D, F, G, H, M, and N are symmetrical. Check drawings for accurate symmetry or accurate lines of symmetry.

Page 126

Answers may vary here. Initially it looks as if all figures are symmetrical except: the flag, the shoe, the boxing mitt, stopwatch, hockey stick, and glove.

The stopwatch is symmetrical if dials and side gizmo are ignored.

The shoe might be if sliced 3-dimensionally by length.

The hockey stick, boxing mitt, and glove could also be if approached 3-dimensionally with a lengthwise split.